MGA
The Complete Story

Other Titles in the Crowood AutoClassics Series

MGA

The Complete Story

David G. Styles

First published in 1995 by
The Crowood Press ltd
Ramsbury, Marlborough
Wiltshire SN8 2HR

Paperback edition 2001

British Library Cataloguing in Publication Data
A catalogue record for this book is available from the
British Library.

ISBN 1 86126 466 6

Picture Credits
Photographs supplied by: the archives of *Automobile
Quarterly*, Geoff Barron and Nick Cox of the MGA Register
of the MG Owners Club, LAT Photographic, the National
Motor Museum, Beaulieu, Paradise Garage, Sotheby's and
the author.

Road Test data reproduced by kind permission of *The
Autocar & Motor*, *Car & Driver* and *Road & Track*. Other
illustrations from *Autosport* and Moss Europe Ltd.

Dedication
To my wife, Ann, my daughter, Emma and my son Philip,
for their continued tolerance of my writings.

Typeset by Phoenix Typesetting, Ilkley, West Yorkshire
Printed and bound in Great Britain by The Bath Press

Contents

Acknowledgements

A lot of people have given help and support in the creation of this book since I was invited to write it. I'm especially grateful to Tony Bailey and Peter Samuels, of MG specialists the MG Machine, for the benefit of their experience in compiling parts of the book and for leading me to others who helped with their particular knowledge. Geoff Barron, of the MGA Register, and Nick Cox were both helpful in the search for pictures, as were John Baldwin of Paradise Garage and Rupert Banner of Sotheby's. Adrian Wood of Moss Europe Ltd kindly allowed the reproduction of material from that company's MGA parts catalogue, as well as providing important data on dates of changes.

Jonathan Stein, Publishing Director of the quality American publication *Automobile Quarterly,* is also a long-standing enthusiast of MGAs and is perhaps one of the leading authorities on MGA coupés. Thanks to Jonathan's generosity, a number of pictures from the archive of *AQ* appear in this book: then he also kindly read the manuscript and gave numerous pointers on detail, correcting several errors of fact on the way.

I have driven several MGAs, though have never owned one. It is a car for which I have a strong liking and I hope very much that the fruits of my research will result in growing enthusiasm for MGAs worldwide. If I've missed anyone out of these acknowledgements, then I publicly apologize. Indeed, my final 'thank you' is to all those unnamed people who have helped in some way and to MGA enthusiasts everywhere.

Introduction

The MGA heralded a totally new age for the MG Car Company, more so than anyone could ever have dreamed back in the days when Syd Enever and John Thornley were battling for approval to put the new model into production in the wake of the Nuffield/Austin merger which brought about the British Motor Corporation. Few could have realized the profound effect this new model would have on the way of life at MG's Abingdon factory, for such would be the popularity of this new model that it would be produced in greater numbers than all the previous MG models built at Abingdon put together.

Much has been said about the politics that surrounded the pace of the MGA's development, it being claimed in some quarters that Leonard Lord, Chairman of the Austin Motor Company and of the new BMC, was determined to 'teach Abingdon a lesson' by approving funds for the development of the Austin Healey 100 sports car ahead of MG's Project EX175. Whether that was a consideration in the chairman's mind or not is irrelevant in fact, as the chronological sequence of events supports the business logic of the decisions made at that time. Austin had already made a serious strike at the important US market with the A90 Atlantic without success. Discussions had already

begun with Donald Healey about the production of an Austin/Healey sports car and the design was well under way by the time that EX175 was put before the board. Austin was also engaged in early discussions with the Nash Motor Company in the United States, which ultimately led to the production at Longbridge of the Metropolitan. Dollars were more important to Leonard Lord at that time than petty politics, though it is reliably said that he was not averse to taking the odd snipe at those of the old Nuffield empire when the opportunity arose.

Whatever the politics, they were ultimately overcome and the MGA did reach production, to become one of the most sought-after classics of Abingdon today. The under-powered 1500, the misunderstood Twin-Cam and the excellent 1600s combined to produce over 100,000 examples of one of the prettiest British sports cars of its era. The success of this model led to the even greater sales success of the model which followed it, but such is the esteem in which I hold the MGA that I believe it was not until 1995, with the introduction of the MGF, that a car bearing an Octagon badge was produced that could claim to be a worthy successor to the MGA. If this book serves to prolong the life of even one MGA, then the writing of it will have been worth while.

MGA EVOLUTION – SIGNIFICANT DATES, NAMES AND EVENTS

1949   Introduction of the MG TD Midget, the first independent front suspension MG sports car.
George Phillips enters his much-modified TC Midget in the Le Mans 24 Hours.

1950   George Phillips enters Le Mans for a second time and secures a Class Second.
Phillips approaches Syd Enever at MG to produce a streamlined body for a TD Midget in preparation for a third entry in the Le Mans 24 Hours.

1951   Abingdon allocates Project Number EX175 to TD Midget successor.
Agreement to produce special streamlined body on TD Midget chassis for George Phillips's third Le Mans entry. Allocated Project Number EX176.

1952   British Motor Corporation created out of merger of Austin Motor Company and Nuffield Corporation.
John W. Thornley appointed General Manager of MG Car Company.
EX175 placed before Longbridge-based BMC Board for approval – rejected.

1953   MG TF Midget succeeds TD model.
EX179 record-breaker built, using basic chassis concept adopted for MGA.

1954   Capt G.E.T. Eyston secures eight new International Class F speed records with EX179.

1955   MG TF Midget 1500 succeeds TF in attempt to restore flagging sales.
EX182 cars appear at Le Mans, then at RAC Tourist Trophy Race.
Announcement of MGA 1500 Roadster.

1956   MGA 1500 Coupé introduced.
Peco supercharger & HRG-Derrington cylinder head kit for MGA announced.
EX179 raises 10-Mile International Class F Record to 170.15mph powered by Twin-Cam engine.

1957   Five new International Class F Speed Records set with EX181, driven by Stirling Moss and Phil Hill.

1958   Introduction of MGA Twin-Cam in Roadster and Coupé forms.
Judson supercharger kit introduced in USA for MGA 1500.

1959   MGA 1600 Mark I announced in Roadster and Coupé versions.

1960   MGA 1600 De Luxe version introduced.
MGA Twin-Cam discontinued.

1961   MGA 1600 Mark II released in Roadster and Coupé versions with Standard and De Luxe options.

1962   MGA discontinued at Chassis Number 109071.
MGA (Project ADO23) announced to the public to succeed MGA.

1 Out with the Old, In with the New

The initials 'MG' stand for the words 'Morris Garages', an Oxford-based motor dealership established by William Morris, founder of the motor manufacturing company, Morris Motors. Like most distributorships of its kind, it offered specially bodied cars which would appeal to a select market. In the Morris Garages case, these were two and four seat variations of mostly open bodies on otherwise standard Morris chassis. With the arrival on the scene of a man named Cecil Kimber, this was all to change.

BIRTH OF THE MIDGET – MG'S MOST FAMOUS MODEL

Cecil Kimber's company built sporting cars using an extensive list of Morris car components. The first MG Midget, the 'M' Type, introduced in April 1929, was a small two-seat sports car which used the engine and other mechanical components of the contemporary Morris Minor, combined with a wooden-framed, fabric-covered body. It placed sporting motoring within reach of many people who would otherwise never have been able to afford it and, of course, provided the foundation of an enviable racing career for the MG name.

The 'M' Type Midget was not designed for racing at the outset; it was intended only to be a sporty road car, aimed at a particular sector of the market. However, its sporting potential was soon seen by those who built it and those who bought it. It was the 'M' Type

MG's 'M' Type was only ever intended to be a 'fun' car, with few pretensions to being a racer. But its performance and durability were major factors in placing the MG name among Britain's all-time great names of motor sport.

which raised the curtain on MG's racing career, three cars being run in the 1929 Junior Car Club's High Speed Trial. Three 'M' Types won the Team Prize in the 1930 JCC Double Twelve Hours Race at Brooklands and won the Team Prize ahead of the Austin team, the only other team to finish intact. Shortly after the Double Twelve, a Midget ran in the Le Mans 24 Hours Race, entered by Captain Francis Samuelson and driven by him in company with F. R. Kindell. The car's engine suffered a broken oil pipe, with the result that it was forced to retire after eight hours, having run at 55mph (90km/h). Samuelson did no more than have the engine repaired at Abingdon, then entered his car for the Spa-Francorchamps 24 Hours Race two weeks after Le Mans. In this race, he and his co-driver not only finished the race, they came fifth in the 1100cc Class at an average race speed of 47mph (75km/h).

SERIOUS RACERS

After the 'M' Type came the purpose-built 'C' Type Midget, a car built specifically for racing (whereas the 'M' Type was originally not). Being built as a racing car did not prevent it being offered for sale to private entrants, thirteen of whom took 'C' Types to the start line at the 1931 JCC Double Twelve. The first five places in the race went to Midgets, which resulted in 'C' Types going to the Irish Grand Prix, where they took the first three places. Then to the Nurburgring, followed by the 1931 RAC Tourist Trophy Race, with more successes. R.T. Horton scored the supercharged 'C' Type's last major success with a win in the 1932 BRDC 500 Miles Race at Brooklands, averaging 96.29mph (155.03km/h) for the race distance – pretty remarkable for a 750cc engine.

The 'C' Type ('Montlhery') Midget had been based on a record-breaking variant of the 'M' Type. That record breaker had been

This is a 'C' Type Midget with so-called 'Montlhéry' radiator cowl, taking part in an event in the 1970s.

The J2 Midget was the car which did most to popularize the MG sports car range among young enthusiasts and was the car most often associated with the term 'boy racers'.

tested and run at Montlhery, which explains the name 'Montlhery'. This magnificent little car was followed by the 'J' Type Midget, the car that did more for the 'boy racer' brigade than any other and the model which put MG into the league of serious car makers, bringing the company nearer to volume production than any model hitherto. Although to such companies as Ford or Austin, or even Morris, the MG Midget was certainly not a mass-produced car, it did represent the largest scale of production the Abingdon firm had ever undertaken.

'J' Type Midgets brought glory to MG too, with the supercharged J3 and J4 models which followed the production J2. The new squat style of the 'J' Types was to become the hallmark of MGs, with their characteristic square radiators, cutaway doors and slab-

shaped fuel tanks. The J4 was the pure racing version of the 'J' Types, with a lightweight doorless version of the road-going sports body and Powerplus supercharger to give it the potential for winning races, which it did admirably.

First of the J4s to leave Abingdon went to the famous MG racer, Hugh Hamilton, who promptly took his new charge to the Nurburgring, where it won its class and broke the lap record in the Eifelrennen of 1933. Sadly, in the following year, Hamilton was to lose his life in the Swiss Grand Prix whilst driving his J4. But the 1933 Tourist Trophy Race was the highlight of both Hamilton's and the J4's racing careers when, after a superb drive, the little car ended the race only forty seconds behind the winning MG K3 Magnette, driven by no less a driver

The K3 Magnette probably did more for the international reputation of MG than any other pre-World War Two model, winning MG's first RAC Tourist Trophy Race (in 1933) and then performing well in that year's Mille Miglia, winning the 1,100cc Class. This picture shows the 1934 model K3, with the long tail.

than the immortal Tazio Nuvolari. Hamilton's Midget ran this gruelling race at an average speed of over 73mph (118km/h).

THE LAST OHC MIDGET

Last of the line of overhead cam-engined Midgets was the 'P' Type, a design which followed the lines of the 'J' Types, though had an extra 3in (76mm) in the wheelbase, largely to accommodate the slightly longer engine which now had three main bearings. The 'P' Type was MG's answer to the challenge from Singer, whose 'Nine Sports' and 'Le Mans' models were beginning to eat into the market space occupied by MG and Austin. Cecil Kimber had wanted to win the Rudge Whitworth Biennial Cup at Le Mans for years and, in the process of establishing a track record for the 'P' Type, three PA Midgets were entered for the 1935 Le Mans 24 Hours Race, all driven by ladies. They didn't win the Rudge Whitworth Cup (Aston Martin did), but they did achieve their average speed goal of 53mph (85km/h) and the

only pit-stop repair was for the replacement of a tail-light bulb.

The PB Midget succeeded the PA, with a larger engine, but then in 1936, greater centralized control within the Nuffield Organisation brought rationalization and MG's overhead camshaft disappeared. After a period of producing some very expensive racing cars – the six cylinder-engined Magnettes and such Midgets as the immortal 'Q' Type and 'R' Type, it was decided in 1936 to introduce a new low-cost MG two-seater. After all, the single-seat racing 'Q' Type had been offered for sale at £750, a price which, whilst most probably coming nowhere near to recovering its production cost, was a fortune to the average enthusiast, to whom £150 was a fair price for a small sports car. There was a need for MG to return to that marketing concept.

THE NEW GENERATION

The TA Midget was the car which heralded the return to the inexpensive sports car

The PA Midget was announced in 1934, growing into the PB in 1935 to combat mounting opposition from Singer.

The first pushrod-engined Midget was the TA, seen here in chassis form. It became the TB before the outbreak of war.

Cecil Kimber (1888–1945)

Born in London on 12 April 1888, Cecil Kimber was the son of a printing machinery manufacturer. His father moved to Lancashire when Cecil was about eight years old. He acquired his education from Stockport Grammar School, leaving to join the parental printing ink business. Interest in things mechanical began in the world of two wheels, when he bought a single-cylinder Rex motor cycle, which was followed by a V-twin 7hp variant of the same make. Astride a borrowed Rex, he was involved in a collision with a car, the consequence of which was that he almost lost his right leg; the compensation from this incident started him on a career on four wheels.

Kimber's first car was a Singer Ten, in which he drove around the Manchester area on business and pleasure. Came the First World War and, because of his injured right leg, he was exempted from military service. A family disagreement over investment in the business caused Cecil to move to Sheffield with his new bride, the former Irene Hunt, to take up a post with Sheffield Simplex, his first job in the motor industry.

A year later came a move to Thames Ditton, in Surrey, to join AC Cars as their buyer, from whence he moved again, just before the end of the war, to Birmingham to join E. G. Wrigley, makers of steering gear, transmissions and axles, and suppliers to Morris Motors. As William Morris was consolidating the foundations of his future empire, and as Wrigley's was approaching its own demise, Cecil Kimber hopped from one to the other in a timely move to become sales manager of Morris Garages. This was the path to success, albeit as the consequence of an unfortunate incident in which the General Manager of Morris Garages, William Morris's old friend Edward Armstead, resigned his position and committed suicide, leaving Morris little alternative than to appoint Cecil Kimber as General Manager.

That was 1922. Kimber lost no time in creating special bodywork for the Morris Oxford to make it a cut above its mass-produced counterpart. So successful was the venture that he was soon asking prices one-third above those of the regular production of the MG Car Company in 1927. Upon MG's move to Abingdon on Thames in 1929, Kimber resigned as General Manager of Morris Garages Limited to devote his whole time to the new business, which became the MG Car Company Limited in July 1930, with Sir William Morris as Governing Director and Cecil Kimber as Managing Director. MG was becoming a force to be reckoned with.

pioneered by MG with the 'M' Type Midget. The TA was now to make maximum use of Morris parts (no more Wolseley engines for MG), so producing a sports car with a price within the reach of young enthusiasts. The marketing ploy of 'catch 'em while they're young and you'll have 'em for life' had not escaped MG or Nuffield and the theory was that if youngsters enjoyed their MGs, they would graduate to other Nuffield cars as they left their sporting youth behind on the inevitable path to motoring maturity.

The TB Midget succeeded the TA in 1939, but was in production for only a very short period, as the onset of the Second World War suspended private car manufacture for over six years. This meant that the Abingdon factory was to be occupied with the maintenance and repair of guns and battle tanks, as well as manufacturing aircraft components. With the return of peace, the first TC Midgets were built before the end of 1945, over a thousand more leaving the factory in 1946, despite

the controls imposed by the Ministry of Supply on raw materials. Exports were to be the key to MG's post-war revival and so the TD was developed, going into production in 1949.

MG's TD Midget was based on the 'Y' Type saloon chassis, which was the first production MG to employ independent front suspension. Indeed, the basic design of that front suspension is instantly recognizable to an MGA owner (even the later MGBs bore more than a passing resemblance), as the design was almost unchanged through the TF to the MGA. And of course, the rack and pinion steering which went with that i.f.s. made it so much more economical to build both right- and left-hand-drive cars, catering for home and export markets. The TD was positively aimed at the North American market, with right-hand-drive exports going to the African continent and Australasia.

Both the TC and the TD were extensively raced at club level throughout the world and perhaps nowhere were MGs seen in greater

The TC Midget brought MG sports car motoring back to life after the end of World War Two and many prominent race and rally drivers 'cut their teeth' on a TC.

The TD was next in the development line of MG Midgets and was the first MG Midget to be fitted with stud-mounted disc wheels as standard, instead of centre-lock wires.

numbers at Club events than in the United States of America. The Sports Car Club of America's racing records are littered with MG wins, both on the west coast and in the north east, where these little cars were most popular. Australia and New Zealand also saw MGs winning and they became quite popular competitors in South Africa, too. But the success of MG in these markets brought envious adversaries, who were quick to trade on MG's success.

NO LONGER A MIDGET

EX176 was a special-bodied TD Midget built for a motor racing photographer named George Phillips for the 1951 Le Mans. Phillips had already raced a TC Midget with considerable success and had fielded that car in the French classic in 1950, though that time without success. He was convinced that, with a streamlined body on his car of reduced frontal area, he could do much better and so approached Abingdon to tell them so.

The result of George Phillips' pressures on

the factory was EX176, a new body designed on the TD chassis to make the most of the limited power output of the TD engine. The car was very much lower than the conventional MG Midget and had fully enveloping bodywork, with a low sloping radiator grille. It was quite similar to the car which was finally to succeed the Midget, though not for a while yet.

UMG400 was the registration number of EX176 and George Phillips spent a great deal of time road-testing the car before his trip to the Sarthe circuit. Finally, the day came and off to Le Mans went car, driver and lots of spares. In practice, the car performed well and, whilst the competition at that year's race was such that the MG had no hope of winning overall, it could have stood a chance in the Index of Performance and in its class. The bodywork was so well designed and streamlined that, in the race, EX176 put up better lap speeds than the supercharged pre-war K3 Magnettes had done and lapped distinctly faster than the published maximum speed of a production TD Midget. However, having proved that, after three

George Phillips's TC Midget was modified to look like this for his first attempt at Le Mans in 1949. He drove the same car to a Class second place in 1950, then graduated to his TD. Phillips was Autosport *chief photographer at that time.*

By the end of 1950, George Phillips had so impressed the Abingdon team that Syd Enever was persuaded to design a new streamlined body for Phillips's TD Midget, to be raced at Le Mans in 1951. This body was given the works experimental number EX176 and clearly was the precursor of the line adopted for the next generation MG sports car, the MGA.

The TF Midget was a 'facelifted' TD aimed at holding the important American market for MG, pending the approval of a new model.

hours the engine failed, putting Phillips and MG out of the race.

After further chassis development and refinement of the body line, Syd Enever, MG's Chief Designer, decided that here was a car worth putting forward to the new Longbridge-based board of the British Motor Corporation for production, as a logical successor to the TD Midget. However, economics and politics were to rule the day and the project was overruled in favour of the Austin Healey 100/4, a Longbridge-based design which had been under development before the creation of the British Motor Corporation.

In actual fact, the Austin Healey was in the over-2-litre sports car category, positioned in a market slot above the MG and aimed at succeeding the Healey Silverstone, which was long in the tooth now and had always been too expensive to have a wide

appeal, especially in the all-important North American export market. The Austin-weighted management offered the view that a new Midget would be more in keeping with the public's perception of the MG image, whilst they were anxious to establish the Austin Healey as the sporting flagship of the newly formed British Motor Corporation, so helping to reinforce the name of the Corporation, and Austin, in the US market. Views have been expressed also that BMC Chairman Leonard Lord, formerly Austin Chairman, wanted to favour Austin at the expense of the old Nuffield companies and so held funding back from MG and others. All this meant that another Midget had to be produced.

The final stop-gap car between the 'T' series of MG sports cars and a whole new generation of Abingdon-built two-seaters was the TF 1500, a beautifully restored example of which is seen in this picture at the MG Car Club's Diamond Jubilee celebrations at Silverstone in 1990.

TF – THE FINAL MIDGET

As sales of the TD Midget began to fall, especially in North America, so the TF was introduced. Thanks to the decision not to pursue the development of EX176, at least for the time being, a facelift of the TD would be as far as the economics would allow development to go. So would be born the TF Midget, with lowered body line and detail changes, including the sloping radiator grille and, for the first time on an MG, a pressurized cooling system. Even though, by 1955, a 1500cc engine was installed in the TF, it was not viewed as a sales success.

Starting as a 1,250cc-engined 'streamlined' development of the TD, the TF Midget's primary objective was to hold US and Canadian sales long enough to allow the completion of a totally new car. The TF was, to all intents and purposes, a TD lowered and 'smoothed out'. Apart from being the first MG to use a pressurized cooling system, it was also the first MG production two-seater to feature headlamps faired into the front wings and to have sloping radiator. Yet it had

The Austin Healey 100/4 was the first sports car from the new BMC empire to enter production, going on sale more than two years ahead of the MGA. Powered by a larger engine, it was not set as a direct competitor (or alternative) to the Abingdon car. This example is the elegant 100M model with louvred bonnet.

a link with the past, in the form of an instrument panel which bore more than a passing resemblance to a pre-war MG, the WA Saloon. But the more streamlined form of the TF made it less of a true 'square-rigged' MG and so, whilst some 30,000 TDs were built, fewer than 10,000 TFs left Abingdon in its near three year production life, even despite the slight performance improvement of the 1,500cc engine.

Finally, before the inevitable decision was taken to kill off the TF, the senior management at Longbridge called for a review of the EX175 project and then acceded to the development and introduction of a new MG model, which would come to be known as the MGA. Of course, the body line was based on EX176, which was extensively revamped to take account of developments in styling and the needs of production tooling.

LEAD-UP TO THE MGA

Numerous conclusions have been drawn about the decision to defer the development of the car which was to become the MGA, but, whatever the emotions, it must be accepted that the decision was based upon commercial logic which had good foundations, even though they might not have best suited the preferences of MG enthusiasts. The Austin Healey 100/4 was a logical successor to the Healey Silverstone, as well as being a head-on competitor for the Triumph TR2 in the prized US and Canadian markets for British sports cars. Furthermore, the Austin Healey was capable of taking a larger engine, which would enable it to move further up the market and away from the MGA when that car did arrive.

The design outline of the Healey 100/4 was also light-years ahead of the TD Midget; it would use many production Austin components (just as the Triumph TR2 used many production Standard components) and would serve to enhance the developing relationship between Austin and the Nash Corporation in the United States (leading to the Metropolitan) after the inability of the A90 Atlantic to capture sufficient market share for Longbridge. Then, of course, it must be remembered that the power of management in the newly formed British Motor Corporation polarized towards Longbridge, which plant was looking to seal a relationship in the

United States, where it saw a huge export potential.

Bearing in mind the fact that the Austin Healey 100/4 project was already well advanced by the time BMC came into being, and that it was felt there wasn't enough money in the pot to develop two British sports cars under the same corporate roof for sale side-by-side in North America, the Healey probably really was the logical choice for development at the time. Furthermore, commercial intelligence sources reliably told of the impending growth of domestic sports car products in the United States, which would ultimately crystallize in the dual forms of the Chevrolet Corvette and the Ford Thunderbird – hardly true sports cars to the European mind, but the Corvette was to prove to be a car to be taken seriously. In this light, the Austin Healey was the ideal choice for BMC, as it was a chunky, but aerodynamically clean, car with that potential for a bigger engine.

Once the Austin Healey was developed and established, there would be time, in the view of BMC corporate management, to develop another sports car which could compete in a different sector of the market. The Healey was now destined to become the 100/6 and position itself even above the Triumph TR models, cutting straight into the Corvette/Thunderbird market, as well as taking on such European competition as the bigger, and much more expensive, Alfa Romeos (the 2000 and 2600 Spyder) and BMW. MG's development model would now be pitched at the smaller end of the market, competing with such cars as the Porsche 356, the Alfa Romeo Giulietta Spyder and other imports – again, much more expensive models. So, whilst the gestation period of the MGA was prolonged, it was with good cause and

EX175 was the designation given to the prototype MGA. This is the second prototype car, shown modified for evaluation as a potential record breaker in 1953/54. The general line of the MGA is now clear, though there were still minor modifications of detail to be made before the definitive MGA saw the light of day.

The record breaker EX179, photographed at Bonneville, was significant to the MGA story because its chassis lent much to the production MGA.

perhaps there was some benefit to be derived from the wake of the Austin Healey's success and the stark contrast between the appearance of the TF and the MGA when it finally did arrive on the scene.

THE MGA – AND A LEGEND – IS BORN

Given that George Phillips' TD Midget EX176 ran as long ago as 1951, it is perhaps a little surprising that the design outline remained viable for so long, for it was four years and two experimental cars later that the MGA finally saw the light of day. It should be pointed out at this stage that MG's experimental project number EX175 had been issued for the development of a successor to the TF Midget prior to the construction of EX176, though EX176 did appear first. So,

the chain of development goes from EX176 to EX175 to EX179 to EX182 and then to the production MGA.

The pattern of development is not quite as simple as the linear train of models indicates, however, as the primary task of EX175 was to develop the styling of the new model. A wide chassis frame was used for this model, but the ultimate development of that frame can better be credited to EX179, a Class F record breaker. It is hardly coincidence, though, that Syd Enever's chassis frame for EX175 was virtually identical to EX179. The body of EX175 was very close in line to the production car, though it bore a telltale link with the past, in the form of a power bulge which concealed an XPEG engine, pending the decision to use the BMC 'B' Series.

EX179 was logically the next phase in the development of the new MG two-seater, for it

Despite being built before the Second World War, 'Goldie' Gardner's record-breaker, EX135, lent much of its shape to EX179.

was this car which featured the chassis that was to develop into EX182, the definitive prototype of the MGA. EX179 was built as an International Class F record breaker for Captain George Eyston and in August 1954 it set eight new records. The low, wide box-section chassis frame confirmed the design concepts of the EX175 frame and, as a result, was remarkably similar to the chassis of EX182, which was then revised only slightly to accommodate manufacturing convenience in the production of the MGA.

For those not 'in the know', especially MG buffs in North America, it seemed odd, even incongruous, that MG could produce such streamlined record breakers as EX135 (a pre-Second World War K3 Magnette with offset drive-line built for Captain George Eyston and later re-bodied by Reid Railton for a successful run at a 200mph (320km/h)-plus 1,100cc record by Lieutenant-Colonel A. T. G. 'Goldie' Gardner in 1939) and EX179 (the logical successor to EX135), whilst its production sports cars remained positively 'square-rigged', even if slightly tempered by the lower lines of the TF. EX135, incidentally, was also the car which set new 1,500cc records using an XPAG engine in 1951.

So, after a lot of political to-ing and fro-ing, it was finally decided at Longbridge that the time had come for the authorization of a new MG to replace the TF Midget, which was far from a sales success. EX175 was now to be developed into a production model at last. It was decided that three prototypes would be built for entry in the 1955 Le Mans 24 Hours Race and that the press would be invited to a test session after that race. Thus was born EX182 and with it, the decision to end the train of 'T' Series Midgets. It was to be a case of: 'Out with the old and in with the new'. . .

2 MGA Marks the End of an Era

The prototype from which the MGA was developed was finally approved by Leonard Lord, Chairman of the British Motor Corporation in 1953 and so EX182 was to be born out of the lines of EX176. Whilst there was much resentment around at the time that the original presentation of EX176 was rejected in favour of the Austin Healey 100/4, it has subsequently been generally accepted that the delay was actually a blessing in disguise, since it enabled the Abingdon design team to opt for the newly introduced BMC 'B' Series engine as the power unit for the new car.

Introduction of the new model would take place in 1955 and the ultimate model designation was decided to be the MG 'UA' Type, abandoning the name 'Midget' now, as it was thought no longer appropriate. Unfortunately, the name 'Magnette' had already been allocated to a saloon car, otherwise it might have been the ideal name for what was to be recognized as a revolutionary new design in MG terms.

Three development prototypes were to be built of this new model and, with the decision being made that the British Motor Corporation would return to motor sport, Syd Enever's team went to work with the clear objective of building three cars for entry in the 1955 Le Mans 24 Hours Race in June. Thus was born EX182.

EX182 GOES TO LE MANS

The three prototype cars built under MG's experimental number EX182 were prepared as carefully as any pre-war racing MGs had ever been prepared. The task in hand was to perform as well as they possibly could, recognizing that they had little prospect of an outright win against such opposition as Aston Martin, Ferrari, Jaguar, Maserati and Mercédès-Benz.

It was generally accepted that, by 1955, Le Mans had become something of a 'sports car-bodied grand prix' type of race. Using the category of prototype, a Grand Prix single-seater could be adapted to accept a sports car two-seat body and entered legitimately to compete against genuine production sports cars. Mercédès-Benz even fitted a hydraulically operated air brake/spoiler behind the driver to aid speed reduction without wearing out conventional brakes. This really was going to the extreme, but such was the flexibility of Le Mans rules at the time.

The cars which would be likely true competitors for the MGs were such as the Porsches, Oscas, the 1500cc Kieft and the single Connaught. That said, none of these were production cars in the accepted sense, though the Porsches came nearest, in that most of those entered were privately owned and the Spyder was a car offered for sale, though it was certainly not a conventional production car for everyday street use, whereas the MG EX182 cars were literally the precursors of a volume production model.

The body line, mechanical specification, radiator grille, headlamp positions and general appearance of the EX182s were all transferred pretty faithfully to the

EX182 was the near-final form of the MGA, the three development prototypes being entered for the 1955 Le Mans 24-Hours Race and then the Ulster Tourist Trophy Race before the model entered production.

production MGA. Additions to the production model, of course, included a road-going windscreen, carpets and full interior trim, conventional fuel capacity, a full second seat and bumpers front and rear. But in general terms, the MGs and Lance Macklin's Austin-Healey were probably the closest thing to production cars entered for the 1955 Le Mans.

A RECORD RACE

A race of record speeds was expected that year, with the battle focusing on Castellotti's 4.4-litre Ferrari, Fangio's Mercédès-Benz and Hawthorn's 'D'-Type Jaguar. From the beginning, Castellotti set the pace and within an hour of the start, Hawthorn and Fangio were continuing a rivalry which had

begun at the 1953 French Grand Prix, though Hawthorn was now driving a British car with Ivor Bueb and, despite lying third at this early stage of the race, was bent on winning. Mike Hawthorn did win that Le Mans, but not in the way he would have wanted, for a terrible accident marred the event.

At around 6.30 on the Saturday evening of the race, Hawthorn had lapped the French driver, Levegh, in a Mercédès-Benz, and Lance Macklin in his Austin Healey, then pulled into the pits. Macklin swerved to avoid hitting Hawthorn's car, as he clearly thought it too close for comfort, and Levegh, in an attempt to avoid the Austin Healey, which had positively 'shut the door' on him, ran into the retaining bank and shot over it, hitting the concrete wall which bordered the pedestrian tunnel through to the pits, the car splitting up as it struck the wall. The front suspension and wheels flew off the car in one direction, the engine in another, each scything through the crowded area to leave a death toll of over eighty people, including the innocent Frenchman. At about the same time as this terrible accident, which in more modern times would almost certainly have caused the abandonment of the race, news came in that Dick Jacobs had overturned his MG at Maison Blanche and was badly injured.

In all the confusion, it seems almost unbelievable that the race would have continued, though Alfred Neubauer withdrew the Mercédès-Benz team later that evening and all the Ferraris dropped out with various failures. This put Hawthorn into the lead and that was where he and Ivor Bueb stayed to the end of the race, followed by Peter Collins' and Paul Frère's Aston Martin into a magnificent second place.

Porsche were expected to do well in the 1500cc Class and well they did, taking the first three places in the Class and finishing fourth, fifth and sixth overall into the bargain, a pretty astonishing feat against cars with twice the engine capacity. The three Bristol 2-litres were seventh, eighth and ninth, winning their Class on the way, whilst the Frazer Nash and Osca were tenth and eleventh respectively, with an MG, driven by Lockett and Miles in twelfth place. The other MG, driven by Lund and Waeffler came home in seventeenth place, so the two Abingdon cars had certainly not disgraced themselves in their first ever event – especially one of twenty-four hours duration. They were also awarded the Team Prize, whilst the race speeds were pretty good, too, with Lockett and Miles turning in over 87mph (140km/h) and the Lund/Waeffler car just over 82mph (132km/h), compared with the winner's speed of 107mph (172km/h) plus.

These two cars are Porsche Spyders, pictured here running in the 1955 Le Mans race. Whilst the EX182s were not quite production sports cars, these two were a far cry from the kind of car you would have bought from the showroom.

This cutaway drawing from the pen of Autosport's *Theo Page gives an excellent idea of how close the EX182s were to the production MGA, in this case even down to the pushrod 'B' Series BMC engine.*

No one in the summer of 1955 was ever in any doubt as to who was most likely to win the Le Mans 24 Hours Race – the mighty Mercedes Benz 300SLR, being driven to victory here by J.M. Fangio, partnered by Stirling Moss. This was the pinnacle of sports car design in the mid-1950s.

Dick Jacobs drove this EX182 MG at Le Mans and is seen here coming out of the Esses just ahead of the Glockler/Juhan Porsche. Jacobs later crashed at White House and was seriously injured.

THE TOURIST TROPHY RACE

September 17th was the day on which the RAC Tourist Trophy Race took place at Dundrod. It was a race full of controversy from an organizational point of view, the press being very critical of the ways in which classes were organized, in which information was dispensed to the public and press alike and the 'apology of timber and steel tubing which passed for a grandstand'. For all the criticisms, the race had an exciting entry list consisting of some fifty-five cars, ranging from Mercédès-Benz, Ferrari, Maserati, Jaguar and Aston Martin at the top end, down to Cooper, Connaught, DB, Lotus and, of course, MG at the smaller end of the scale. It was to be a race of 625 miles (1,000km/h) – eighty-four laps of a tortuous circuit which

would certainly sort out the men from the boys!

The MG entry consisted of the two EX182 cars which survived Le Mans intact, plus a third. One was fitted with an experimental twin-cam adaptation of the BMC engine, another with a Longbridge-developed twin-cam and the third had a pushrod 'B' Series engine. One twin-cam car was piloted by Johnny Lockett and Ron Flockhart. The pushrod-engined car was driven by Jack Fairman/P. Wilson while the Lund/Stoop car had the other twin-cam power unit. The Fairman/Wilson car had also been fitted with Girling disc brakes instead of the more conventional drums.

The race was not two laps old before a major incident, in the form of a seven-car shunt, marred the event. It happened near

Deer's Leap and involved two Coopers, a Connaught, a Porsche, a Frazer-Nash, an Austin Healey and the sole Lotus-MG. Two drivers, a well-known competitor of the time named Jim Mayers and a promising new-comer, W. T. Smith, were killed in the crash, whilst Ken Wharton was injured, though fortunately not too seriously. The debris was cleared and the race continued, but in rather sombre mood, just as Le Mans had been.

Shortly after the resumption of racing, Ron Flockhart was getting worried about the performance of his twin-cam unit and made a couple of pit-stops for adjustments to the Weber carburettors, before the engine finally gave up the ghost half way into the race. The Lund/Stoop car also went out of the race, leaving Jack Fairman as the only MG finisher. He crossed the line in twentieth place which, for the car's second outing and in mixed weather, was not a bad result. Mike Hawthorn had once again put up the fastest

lap of the race, but victory this time fell to Juan Manuel Fangio and Karl Kling in their Mercédès-Benz 300SLR.

So it was that MG's new model, the 'MGA', made its debut. It was time now for the public launch of a sports car which was to revive the fortunes of the Abingdon factory and the MG name, to say nothing of the additional boost that the MGA would give to the reputation of the British Motor Corporation itself in its quest for business in North America. Many Americans would soon associate the BMC rosette with Austin-Healey *and* MG.

FIRST OF A NEW LINE

One of the early promotional quotes from the British Motor Corporation in the sales campaign for the new MGA was the phrase: 'First of a new line'. And it really was, for this was

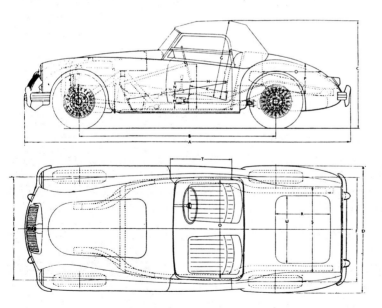

Dimensions

A Overall length, 13 ft. 0 in.
B Wheelbase, 7 ft. 10 ins.
C Overall height, 4 ft. 2 ins.
D Overall width, 4 ft. 10 ins.
E Front track, 3 ft. 11½ ins.
F Rear track, 4 ft. 0¾ in.
G Seat to roof, 3 ft. 1 in.
H Steering wheel to seat back, 1 ft. 5 ins. max., 11 ins. min.
I Floor to centre of steering wheel, 1 ft. 9 ins.
J Seat back to front floor board, 3 ft. 11 ins. max., 3 ft. 5 ins. min.
K Length of seat, 1 ft. 6½ ins.
L Height of seat, 1 ft. 9 ins.
M Floor to edge of seat, 7 ins.
O Length of boot, 2 ft. 6 ins.
P Height of boot, 1 ft. 2 ins.
Q Width at elbows, 3 ft. 8½ ins.
R Length of boot door, 2 ft. 2 ins.
S Width of boot, 3 ft. 3½ ins.
T Width of door opening, 2 ft. 4½ ins.
U Width of boot door, 2 ft. 6 ins.

This outline drawing from the pages of Autosport *shows the principal dimensions of the original MGA 1500.*

The MGA 1500 as it went into production, seen here with the hood up . . .

. . . and here with the hood down.

the first production MG sports car to abandon the boxy line so long associated with the name. The 'square-rigged' look was fine for a car built in the 1930s, even the 1940s, but the mid-1950s really did deserve something more in keeping with the age. Now that 'something' was here, in the form of the MGA.

The decision to use the type name 'MGA', apart from the fact that 'UA' didn't somehow seem too inspiring, was based on that promotional cliche: 'First of a new line'. For hadn't a new generation of MGs just been created in this new model? It was streamlined and of very clean appearance, even more sleek than the Austin Healey 100 and certainly of much cleaner line than the

Triumph TR2. It created as much of a sensation in 1955 as the Jaguar XK120 had on its announcement in 1948. The performance was just as sensational, in that this 1½-litre car was capable of a clean 95mph (155km/h), whereas the Jaguar was really struggling to produce the implied 120mph (195km/h) from an engine more than twice the size.

The new car was to be the last MG built with a separate chassis, the last with a separate body produced by the Morris Bodies plant, the first to have a full-width chassis frame (apart from record-breakers), and certainly the first to have a truly appealing low line that would sell. The engine was the new four-cylinder 1,500cc series 'B' BMC unit of

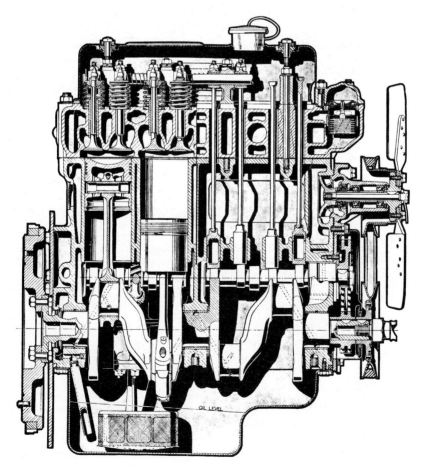

This is the 'B' Series engine in section, as used on the MGA . . .

. . . and here it is in the car, a nicely restored example.

1,489cc, with a bore and stroke of 73.025mm × 89mm. It was still a relatively long-stroke engine, designed in the wake of the old British horsepower-based road licence system, but it was a volume manufactured unit of already proven reliability and performance which, with the two SU carburettors Abingdon fitted, together with a few other slight 'tweaks' produced a power output of 68bhp. Of course, the Magnette saloon was already using this engine in a lesser state of tune, so it was no stranger to Abingdon.

Slightly surprising, perhaps, was the decision to retain drum brakes all round for the MGA, despite Girling discs being tested at the TT on one of the EX182 cars. This was almost certainly a question of production costing rather than specification preference, for the objective facing the manufacturing team at Abingdon was to produce a car which could be sold for under £600. This also meant that disc wheels were specified as standard instead of wires, though wire wheels were an optional extra from the beginning, as was an interior heater (in these days of air-conditioning, that may seem strange, but heaters in most British cars of the day were an optional extra). A radio was also an optional extra, but among the standard features of this car were rack and pinion steering and road-holding which was to be the envy of many another car maker.

SUGAR AND SPICE . . .

The reception given to the new MGA upon its public release was rapturous. The press had barely a bad word for it, most reviewers having already seen it in advance of the motor shows. At the Earls Court Motor Show in October 1955, the public was all over this magic new MG, incredulous at its stream-lined shape and amazed by the price of £595 (plus taxes) asked for the car. Set against the road-holding and handling characteristics of the car, the few criticisms were certainly not about to put buyers off.

Among criticisms offered of the MGA were such things as the limited instrumentation, there being only four dials on the dashboard, the horn button being on the dash instead of in the centre of the steering wheel, the closeness of the hood, the limited head-room, and the small size of the luggage compart-ment. This last point seems a little unfair, when the MGA was the first MG ever to have an enclosed luggage compartment at all! Certainly the luggage space would have been better suited to soft bags of the kind popular in the 1980s and 1990s than to hard suitcases.

More of the MGA's specification became known as more reviews and road tests

appeared and as cars began to find their way into showrooms – though most of the show-rooms into which the cars found their way were in the United States, as export was the paramount priority for all British industry in those days. The nearest many British enthu-siasts came to an MGA for a few years was a brochure.

The widely spaced chassis side members allowed the seats to be placed below the level of the top surface of the chassis, thus giving a much lower seat line than was first seen on EX176, George Phillips' streamlined racer which led to this attractive new sports car. The substantial front end of the chassis had double wishbone and coil spring independent front suspension, whilst the rear suspension consisted of orthodox semi-elliptic springs which passed beneath the rear axle. Double piston lever-action shock absorbers com-pleted the ride control aspect of the suspension. On a wheelbase of 94in (2,388mm) and a front track of 47½in (1,206mm) (the same as the TD and TF Midgets), this near-ideal track/wheelbase ratio of 2:1 combined with a well calculated roll centre and centre of gravity to give the legendary handling for which the MGA became renowned, even on 5.60 × 15 tyres.

Early colours for the MGA included black (a surprisingly attractive colour for such a small car), Orient Red, Tyrolite Green, Glacier Blue and Old English White (another very attractive finish). Interior trims were offered in Red, Green, Grey and White. White upholstery doesn't seem entirely appropriate to a sports car, but if that was what you wanted (it really was a bit 'sugar and spice' though. . .), that was what you got. The only question remaining then was what colour you wanted the hood: Ice Blue or Black?

SAFETY FAST

It is often said that a car can only go as

quickly as it can stop and with a top speed of around 95mph (155km/h), the MGA certainly needed to be able to stop pretty smartly. The original specification of Lockheed drums all round seemed a bit penny-pinching, especially when Triumph was now offering disc brakes on the TR3, but production cost was a key factor and while disc brakes had been tested on one of the EX182 cars in the Tourist Trophy Race, braking performance of the early MGAs left little to chance.

In 'Safety Fast' terms the engine was, of course, a key element in the performance success of the MGA and the BMC Board's delayed approval of the car's development was, from this point of view, a blessing in disguise. It was that delay which allowed the adaptation of the BMC 'B' Series engine to the car in preference to the XPEG engine of the TF Midget. The physical dimensions of the engine were little different, the bore and stroke of the XPEG being 72mm × 90mm, whilst the 'B' Series was 73.025mm x 89mm, making a capacity gain of just 23cc and a power boost of 5bhp for the same engine speed. You might be forgiven for asking then what benefit was conferred on the MGA by the delay in its development production as a result of the availability of the 'B' Series engine.

British Motor Corporation's 'B' Series engine was a free-running unit which proved its performance potential over many years. Before finding its way into the MGA, it had already been installed in the 'Z' Series Magnette Saloon, though the two-seater version was a higher performance variant with an 8.3:1 compression ratio. Fuel was drawn from the rear-mounted 10-gallon (45-litre) tank by means of a single SU electric pump and fed into a pair of 1½in bore SU carburettors. All this resulted in a fuel consumption of 29mpg (9.8l/100km/h), driven hard, and a quoted maximum speed of 96mph (155km/h). Pretty good for the mid-1950s.

But the fundamental benefits of the 'B' Series engine to the MGA lay not in its extra performance potential or its physical size, but far more in its unit cost in manufacture, the wider availability of spares and the resulting improved serviceability. Clearly, too, the 'B' Series would be around for a long time, so providing an opportunity for considerable development. A part of that development potential was demonstrated very early in the life of the MGA by the creation of a twin cam version for use in the EX182 driven by Lockett and Flockhart in the Ulster T.T.

The gearbox in the MGA was a four-speed unit, with synchromesh on second, third and top and selection by means of a short lever mounted in a cast alloy remote control housing. Power into the gearbox was transmitted via a Borg and Beck 8in (203mm) diameter single plate dry disc clutch, whilst power out left the gearbox output shaft to connect to a Hardy Spicer universal coupling and, via the open propeller shaft, went into the BMC 'B' Type three-quarter-floating rear axle carrying a hypoid bevel differential of either 4.3:1 ratio (10/43 standard) or 4.66:1 (9/41 optional). It's fairly easy to see why this streamlined marvel, which incidentally weighed in at under 2,000lb (900kg) fully road-equipped, was capable of coming so close to 100mph (160km/h) with only a 1,500cc engine.

THIS IS A SPORTS CAR?

To the hardy, red-blooded sports car type who was generally associated with ownership of an MG, driving a car which was actually comfortable – even draught-free – was just not an essential ingredient of any new car to come out of Abingdon. In fact, such an idea was almost unheard of, even 'cissy'. But it was a fact of life for this fine revolutionary new MG which was set to establish a whole new tradition in MG lore, indeed in the pattern of small British sports cars.

The windscreen mounting of the MGA (showing the standard seats to good advantage – the reader can also just see the rim of the optional extra woodrim steering wheel).

Equipped with 12-volt electrics, the 'A' had the usual provision of head, side and tail lights, with a red dashboard light (these days it's blue on most cars) to show when the headlights were on main beam. Two batteries were used, one behind each seat in quite an awkward position, as the spare wheel had to be moved from its position in the boot to provide access. Still novel in those days were the self-cancelling flashing direction indicators and the self-parking windscreen wipers, though they were still only single speed.

Other electrical 'goodies' which might make the purist shudder were the options of a radio (yes, even a push-button one, at that) and, wait for it, an interior heater. Now that was surely going just too far! They would be telling us next that the interior of the car was

The neatly mounted tail lights of the original MGA . . .

. . . and the dashboard, showing the odd location of the horn button. This car is a 1500 and is fitted with the optional woodrim steering wheel. The painted metal dash is clear to see.

free of those tantalizing little holes in the bulkhead which ensured those cooling air flows which most people have a funny tendency to call draughts! And, of course, it was. Worse, it had carpets to further improve the creature comforts.

On the positive side for the purist, the car did have little windscreen supports which served also as grab-handles and inside it had a map-light, as well as a dashboard lamp. Instruments were, perhaps, worthy of criticism, on two counts. Firstly, there weren't enough of them and secondly, the speedometer and rev-counter had succumbed to the stylist, in that the digits alternated with marks to show thousands of revolutions per minute, the digits being the even numbers. The speedometer dial was similarly printed and did not compare well with the instruments in, for example, a Jaguar XK140, which also used Smith-manufactured dials under the British Jaeger label. And then the oil pressure gauge and water temperature gauge were combined into a single dial, whilst there was no ammeter at all, the only other dial being the fuel gauge.

The creature comforts of the car included well-framed leather-covered seats which were shaped to ensure, within reason, that the occupants didn't fall out of them as the car was cornered with enthusiasm, remembering that seat belts were almost

This is the view that many drivers of lesser sports cars had of the MGA, a view which shows a clean and compact design which gave good attention to detail.

exclusively an eccentricity of the Scandinavians at that time. A 'comfort pad' (not quite an arm-rest as it was too low) covered the transmission tunnel between the seats and wool carpetting (more fitting for a luxury family car) completed the interior trim. The doors were so panelled inside as to provide a pair of pockets for such things as maps and notebooks, but not much else, and the car was devoid of a glove compartment which, on an open sports car, was something of an omission. Whilst something of an MG tradition, the horn-push was in a rather silly place, on the dashboard instead of in the centre of the steering wheel, as with most cars, regardless of their user category.

Draught-free motoring has been referred to before in these pages, but it is worthy of comment that the upper line of the doors gave considerable comfort, so much so that the driver and passenger could drive along with the hood down in fairly cool weather and still be quite snug inside the car. The heater helped to improve things in lower temperatures, but it was still quite possible to motor in comfort with the hood down in winter, provided it wasn't blowing a blizzard or raining more than just a drizzle.

So, all in all, the benefits of the MGA quite outweighed the shortfalls and, for the owner who delighted in extras, there were such options to be bought ex-factory as windscreen washers (essential and compulsory today), a boot-lid mounted luggage rack (essential if you wanted to take more than overnight luggage), wire wheels (essential if

The car which is claimed in some quarters to have been cribbed by Sydney Enever in his design of the MGA – the Jaguar XK120. The differences in the two designs are self-evident.

*The 1956 Sebring 12-Hours Race saw this team of three MGA 1500s entered –
their first major race in the United States after the introduction of the new model.*

*MGAs approaching completion on the Abingdon production line. This was the
car destined to outnumber every MG sports car ever built to date.*

you wanted to preserve your image as a 'sports car driver'), an HMV push-button radio (fitted where the glove compartment *ought* to have been and a useful accessory, despite the 'sportsman's' derision of the day), and a radiator blind to help keep the engine warm in very cold winter weather. Fog lamps were also optional extras, mounted above the front bumper, along with wheel rim trims and, most usefully, a telescopic steering column. Oddly, a tonneau cover, which most people would have expected to see as a part of the standard specification on a sports car, was an extra, too.

THE END AND THE BEGINNING

For the 1956 motoring season, the Abingdon factory had produced a real winner. This was a car which would compare in style with even the much vaunted Jaguar XK series. It was, in the eyes of many (including the author of this book) a much more attractive car – clean of line and superbly proportioned. It was also comfortable and had the road manners and handling of many sports cars costing three

and four times as much. The new MGA was a true value for money motor car. It was also the end of the line, being the last MG built on a separate chassis and thus the last to receive a body manufactured by the Morris Bodies Division.

This car also scored several firsts for MG. It was, of course, the first production MG sports car with a streamlined body, abandoning for ever the square radiator and the angular body style of the 'T' Series Midgets it succeeded. And, of course, this new car was not a Midget – that model name had, for the time being at least, been abandoned also. For the first time, too, the MGA shared an engine common, in general terms, to a range of other cars built by the British Motor Corporation's group of companies.

The MGA was the first car of a new generation of MGs and many other firsts were to be established before it was succeeded by the MGB, including the introduction of disc brakes, a twin-cam engine, the resulting 100-mph production MG two-seater and the first 100,000 plus production level for a two-seat MG. This was the beginning of a whole new era for the MG name. . .

3 The MGA 1500 on the Road

From the day it first appeared, the MGA received a warm welcome. It was seen by the press of the day as something revolutionary (which, indeed, it was) and by much of the public as the car they had been waiting for. This latter opinion was especially true of the North American market, upon which the British Motor Corporation (and most of the rest of British industry at the time) relied so heavily for its income. And this is most of the point, for the new car was seen by its maker as Abingdon's saviour, which indeed it was, according to the resulting sales figures, as well as being a successor to a line which was now distinctly long in the tooth.

RESTORING THE FAITH IN MG

It almost didn't matter where else the MGA met with success, as long as it did so in the United States of America. It seems strange to contemplate that between 80 and 95 per cent of British engineering exports in the middle 1950s went across the Atlantic – and perhaps stranger to realize that in some cases, that export level represented more than 80 per cent of actual production. It seems sad that successive governments in Britain did not see the point of providing the tax climate that would have encouraged the technological development essential to maintaining that export thrust, thus the prosperity of Britain itself, but such long-term thinking seems not to be the stuff of good political charisma.

From the time the news first came that

there was to be a new MG sports car, with the revelation of the 1955 Le Mans cars and the subsequent invitation to the press to try them out, there was a mixture of surprise, relief and apprehension. The surprise lay in the news that the new car would follow closely the styling of the Le Mans cars which, of course, it did. The relief came from the same news, that it was not to be a further revamped TF Midget, but a new car. The apprehension arose from a nervousness about how reliable the new car would be, using as it did a new engine, albeit one modified at Abingdon under the close scrutiny of Chief Engineer Syd Enever. There was, of course, also the cynical reaction of the so-called purists, who condemned the kind of change represented by the introduction of the MGA as not in keeping with all that was traditional MG. They were either unable or unwilling to appreciate that if the product did not progress, it would not sell and so the maker would die.

Restoring the faith in the product was, therefore, a high priority at Abingdon and the promotion of this elegant new car was as essential to its success as its ability to perform and keep performing. The new BMC power unit was reliable and many other items in the car's specification were recognizable from the TD and TF models. The decision to use carried-over components, notably from the front suspension, was one based on costing efficiency, but it had the spin-off value of allowing the Abingdon team to point out a continuity which established a positive link between the old and the new.

Sydney Enever

Syd Enever started his career in the motor industry as a shop-boy with Morris Garages in Oxford. He wasn't there long before his sketches of cars were noticed and a rare talent for design realized. When the MG Car Company was established at Abingdon, Sydney Enever was recruited to the new team. H.N. Charles, the MG Car Company's Chief Design and Development Engineer, was highly impressed with young Enever's insight and his capacity to produce a complete design idea from a clean sheet of paper.

As the Abingdon factory developed its product range, so Syd Enever made his mark on the product and a significant impression on his employer. Within five years, he was enjoying a remarkable degree of independence for a man with no formal engineering qualifications, but he earned every bit of respect and trust accorded him as he contributed to several of MG's racing car designs before the absorption of MG into the Nuffield empire and the subsequent decision to withdraw from racing in mid-1935 and in the middle of the development of the 'R' Type Midget.

With the reorganization, only two of the old design team were retained at Abingdon, one of whom was Syd Enever. Their remit now was to consult on the styling of the new range of MGs and to lead the design route of the company down the road of using more and more Nuffield-standardized components so as to keep down the production cost, but capitalize on the octagon badge, enlarging the range of interchangeability and reducing service problems as a consequence. A by-product of this policy was that the production MG sports car became a more tractable vehicle for everyday use and so attracted more sales, creating more profit.

After the Second World War, Syd Enever designed a special engine for Lt.-Col A. T. G. 'Goldie' Gardner's record breaker, EX135, to enable it to set a new 750cc record at Jabbeke in 1946, then for the 500cc record in 1948. He designed the body for George Phillips' TD special, EX176, then produced a new chassis to allow the driver to sit lower in the car and there was EX175, the basis of the new MGA, designed in 1952 and finally put into production in 1955. The MGA must be the ultimate hallmark of Sydney Enever's design skills.

The immediate American reaction to the MGA was to be all-important to MG and, fortunately, the US press was euphoric in its reception of the new model. It seems a little surprising that a country so committed to a 'big is beautiful' philosophy, combined with lots of chrome, should take this little British sports car so much to its heart, but it did, especially in California and the north east. That Abingdon had found the courage to abandon the 'halfway house' of the TF had been enough to restore the faith of MG enthusiasts across the water and assure sales.

So, the cynical reaction of the MG traditionalists, who already regarded the TF as a step too far, was countered by the certain sales growth which would come from the US market.

FIRST PRESS REACTIONS

By September 1955 MGAs were being made available to the press for road testing, and their opinions were carefully awaited, both at the factory and in the showrooms, though the showrooms where the car was most readily available were on the western side of the Atlantic. All were soon able to heave sighs of relief, as the views of correspondents were published.

The leading general motoring weeklies in Britain picked their way through the specification of the car, commenting on how much more room there was in the MGA compared with the TF Midget. One correspondent observed the painted instrument panel, indicating that it was simply a

Here's how the rear quarter of the MGA looked – the luggage rack is one of many which were on the market at the time, confirming the small size of the car's boot.

pressing – he clearly expected a wooden dashboard! He did, however, praise the high door line, facilitated by the wider body, so allowing the line to be raised without intrusion on elbow space. Clearly, this correspondent was a traditionalist, only grudgingly accepting MG's finest car yet.

An interesting sign of Abingdon's export aspirations was that one of the first road test MGAs released to the British press was a left-hand-drive car. One journal therefore took the car into Northen Europe for its road test, where they recorded some interesting performance figures. For example, a standing quarter mile in just under 20½ seconds compares very well with most contemporary 1500cc sports cars and, perhaps to put it into perspective, when set against the standing quarter mile of such a car as the 1985 Porsche 911 Cabriolet 3.2's 15.85 seconds, was quite remarkable. On the other hand, the MGA's 0–60mph time was quite unremarkable, at 16 seconds. A diesel powered saloon car of the 1990s is capable of performance of that order.

It can certainly be said that had five-speed gearboxes been in fashion in 1955, the MGA was just the kind of car which would have benefitted from one. The gear ratios in themselves perhaps don't mean too much, but when one looks at the road speeds in the gears, it quickly becomes apparent that the

On the boot of the original MGA was this large chrome three-piece badge set, consisting of the MG octagon and the letters 'MG'.

The simple chrome-plated oval vent badge on the scuttle carried the inscription 'MGA'.

gaps between all four ratios are far too wide, even for a sports car of its day. The maximum in first gear was quoted as 26mph (42km/h), second as 42mph (68km/h), third as 68mph (109km/h) and top speed was just under 98mph (158km/h). Ideally, third needed to be much nearer to top, around 80–85mph (130–135km/h), with second nearer to 70mph (110km/h) and first around double its quoted speed, but that would have necessitated another bottom gear to give around 30mph (48km/h) as its top speed. But then, with only four gears, giving the kinds of road speeds advocated here would have meant that the popular market sector at which the MGA was aimed would have been less enthusiastic, as they would have found the car much more difficult to drive – and the inclusion of a fifth gear would have increased the price well beyond Abingdon's target, though it could have been an optional extra.

FIRST ROAD TESTS OF THE MGA

Our intrepid reporters of the 1950s were certainly impressed with the road-holding and braking of the MGA, though they found a marked improvement in cornering capability as the result of increasing tyre pressures to $26lb/in^2$ ($1.8kg/cm^2$) all round, in preference to the recommended $18lb/in^2$ ($1.3kg/cm^2$) front and $23 lb/in^2$ ($1.6kg/cm^2$) rear. The only surprise in that is the low recommended pressures given by the factory. Having dealt with that, the comfort and performance were said to improve substantially and the braking performance was not reckoned to have been adversely affected by this tyre pressure change. In fact, the 10in drum brakes were thought to give outstanding performance with a minimum of fade, though the factory standard disc wheels would certainly not have helped brake cooling, the air flow through and around wire wheels making that option a worthwhile investment.

Criticism from the domestic press came in only small doses, the afforded leg space being a problem for one tester, who felt he needed a double-jointed right knee in the left-hand-drive car he was testing (it presumably would have been his left in a right-hand-drive car!). Other adverse comments came about the fact that it was difficult to change down from third to second gear (double de-clutching might have solved this) and the cable-operated clutch which, in a left-hand-drive car, would have followed a more tortuous route than in a right-hand-drive version.

John Bolster, reporting for *Autosport*, made no bones about his road test, opening it with a repetition of an old statement: 'The racing car of today is the touring car of tomorrow'. He went on to confirm: ' . . . How true are those oft-quoted words when applied to the new MG', reminding the reader that the chassis had been seen in 1954, in the form of the base of EX179, Captain George Eyston's International Class F record breaker, and that the car itself had been preceded by the EX182 Le Mans MGs.

Now John Bolster was a man who had a reputation for not mincing his words, so for him to be as impressed as he clearly was with the MGA was praise indeed for the car. However, he had his criticisms. For example, he felt the driving position was less than ideal, the seats giving insufficient leg support and being, for him, too upright in posture (another journal had commented that there wasn't adequate support for the lower back, so clearly the seat back-rest was not entirely satisfactory). Bolster went on to criticize the reach to the steering wheel, advocating the optional telescopic steering column as an essential to increase the distance from seat back to steering wheel and thus improve comfort.

The general road-holding again came in

for a good deal of praise, with braking performance receiving similar accolades to those of the other road testers who'd driven the left-hand-drive version – Bolster's test car being a right-hand-drive model. The fly-off hand-brake met with distinct approval and drew the comment from John Bolster that he couldn't understand why all sports car manufacturers did not fit them as standard (it might be said that manufacturers of good sports cars did, MG among them in those days, and still do, though times and preferences change).

Other features of the MGA which drew criticism included the hood, because of the wind noise when erected, so Bolster recommended that the MGA driver kept the hood down, driving with sidescreens erect and using the excellent heater on cool days, except in the most demanding of weather – another opinion which proved to be shared by other correspondents. The headlamps also came in for some 'stick', as our outspoken road tester felt they were only adequate for cruising at 60mph (95km/h), even at that speed preferring an additional spot lamp for unfamiliar roads. This fault seems to have beset many a British sports car down the years, but with the arrival of quartz iodine head- and spotlamp bulbs, the problem can today be dealt with.

THE MGA GOES TO AMERICA – THE FIRST ROAD TEST

Left-hand-drive models of the MGA were in road testers' hands in the United States by the end of 1955 and the first to publish an opinion was *Sports Cars Illustrated* in its December issue. It must be remembered that America's first two 'sports cars', the Chevrolet Corvette and the Ford Thunderbird, were now in existence and whilst no attempt was made to compare these products with the MGA, both were designed and built with an American style of driving, and

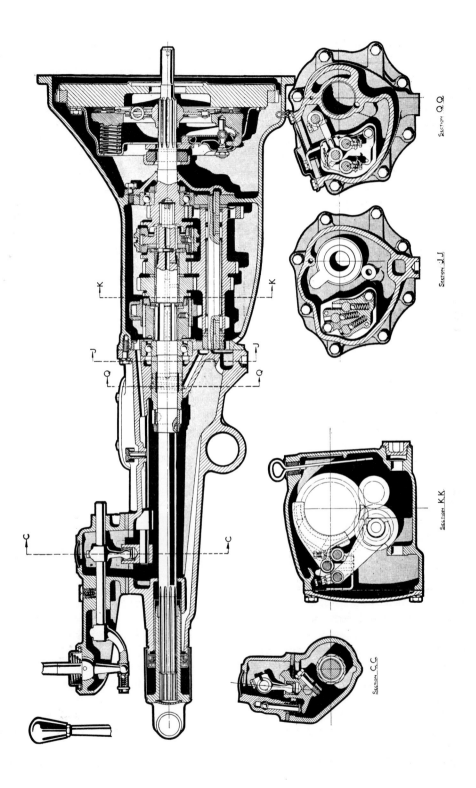

A sectioned view of the MGA gearbox, one of the strong features of the car, which explains why so many specials and kit cars were equipped with the same gearbox.

American road conditions, in mind. The result was that US road testers were more inclined to review the performance of European sports cars in the light of the driving techniques familiar to them and catered for in the domestic products.

This 'conditioning' comes across very clearly in the first American road test of the MGA, where the article opens with the reader 'going for a ride' with the reviewer. Correctly, our road testers observe that there is much more a feeling of sitting 'in' the MGA, rather than the feeling of sitting 'on' its immediate predecessor, the TF Midget (that comment takes you back to the earliest days of motor race reporting, when drivers were described as being 'on' a particular car, rather than 'in' it).

Our 'drive' in the MGA opens with '. . . a quick kick at the clutch . . .', suggesting a driving technique much more at home in a '38 Buick than a 1955 MGA, with the resultant abrupt 'kangaroo' start that was to be expected from such a technique. To give proper credit, however, the American testers do acknowledge that there is a knack and, having acquired it, observe that smooth fast starts are easily possible.

But now we return to the 'conditioned' approach of earlier, where the much higher torque of an American engine is expected, perhaps sub-consciously, to be present in the 1½-litre power unit of the MGA. The 'conditioning' manifests itself in an expectation that the 'B' Series BMC engine is capable of dragging the car smoothly through the rev-range from an engine speed of around 2,300rpm in third gear. No doubt a lump of heavy iron from Detroit would have done that – low speed high geared acceleration in the Corvette was always outstanding, but with over 300lb/ft of torque hauling a car weighing just over a ton it was to be expected. The MGA, on the other hand was only a couple of hundred pounds or so under a ton and was endowed with just over a quarter of the Corvette's torque. Clearly, a slightly different driving technique was called for.

On the positive side, once our intrepid testers had warmed to the car, they had mostly favourable comments to make. They praised the hood for its close fit and complicity with the styling of the car, though reasonably criticized it for the fact that it was not easy for a single person to erect it alone – and certainly not before getting a soaking if the weather changed suddenly. The side-screens, with their sprung bottom flap which kept them closed until driver or passenger wanted to put a hand through, were praised for their closeness of fit and weather protection even without the hood. Again, the comment came forth that the car was better driven with the hood down in all but the most inclement weather, as the wind noise was quite intrusive, though the weather protection from the hood, and the visibility with it erect, were well thought of.

By and large, this first road test came out with the conclusion that the MGA was a fine car in the true British sports car tradition, that its handling was exceptional, even on unmade roads (of which there were several in those days in America, even in California) and that its braking performance was outstanding – drum brakes still being the norm at that time. Acceleration and road speed results compared favourably with domestic road tests already conducted in Britain and generally the MGA was judged to be well worth its $2,190 basic US price.

CONSOLIDATION IN AMERICA

After early comparisons of the MGA with the Porsche Spyder, the Osca and other more expensive European products, as well as with a few Americans that bore no comparison, the British car quickly became accepted in the United States and found itself selling well in the traditionally pro-British New

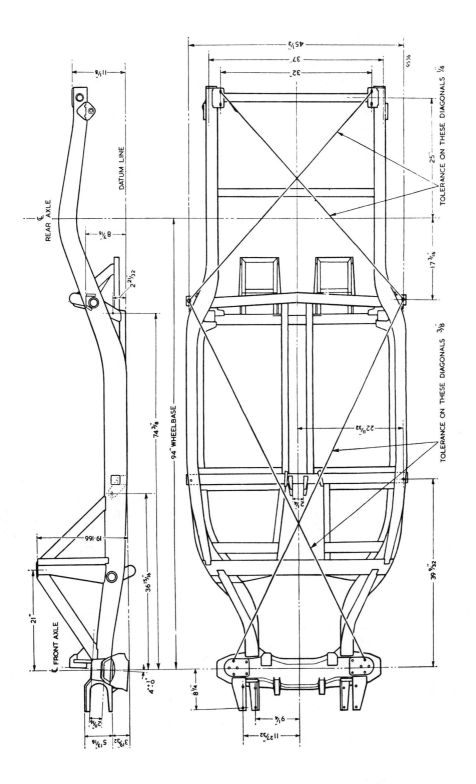

This diagram of the chassis gives a very good indication of the structure and rigidity of the basic MGA design.

England states and in California, the natural target market for open sports cars. Other road testers came into possession of the MGA and were soon publishing their opinions, mostly supportive, mostly objective, but some carrying a few odd observations.

Cars driven on the road, whether in the East Coast states or on the West Coast, produced consistently similar performance and braking figures. There was the odd observation from one correspondent that the car had a tendency to weave at high speed yet he, like all the others, had found the MGA remarkably stable in cross-winds, on dirt roads and on tarmacadam. One has to wonder whether that particular tester's experience was not perhaps the result of his own nervousness of the car at speeds close to its maximum, rather than in any inherent

handling fault which would have been picked up by others if it had existed.

The list of small criticisms of the MGA was building up, and whilst most had some reason behind them, the actual seriousness of the observations had to be a matter in the end for the individual. There was the comment about the gap in steps of seat adjustment, one step taking the driver too close to the steering wheel, the next taking him too far away; clearly a strong case for the telescopic steering column option. There was the valid point that the direction indicator switch cancelled too early, causing potential embarrassment in high-density traffic situations. And then there was the point that the floor-mounted headlight dip-switch was too far away, but nothing here was set to undermine sales which went from around 590 in

That success begets success was certainly proven with the MGA in America. Sales success made more cars available for use in competition, whilst competition successes sold more cars. The lead car of these two in a minor US race meeting is thought to be one of the ex-1956 Sebring vehicles.

North America of the 1,000 or so built in 1955 up to just under 10,600 of the almost 13,400 built in 1956.

UPSIDE AND DOWNSIDE

Despite the encouraging sales figures of the MGA, it has to be remembered that it was being sold into a market that was still starved of good sports cars, especially in the 1500cc class so, as long as it was anywhere near a reasonable performer, it was going to sell. It was a very good performer and so it sold very well, but there were some good grounds for a more seriously critical look at the specification of the car, among them being a close examination of the engine. One journalist took a very close look at the 'B' Series BMC unit and concluded that, whilst it was a positive step forward from the Morris XPEG unit which had powered the TF Midget, this new engine had a few factors which did not work in its favour if the proud new owner wanted to take it racing.

On the plus side, the BMC 'B' Series was lighter than its predecessor and produced an additional 5bhp in production form. It had larger crankpins than the XPEG, but slightly smaller main bearings (forty thousandths of an inch). It was noticed that the big-end caps were offset, so allowing the removal of piston and connecting rod assembly up through the cylinder bore, rather than separating the two and removing the piston upwards and the rod downwards – a very positive plus point for the home tuner/rebuilder. The concave piston crown of the standard engine also meant that there was scope for increases in compression ratio beyond the 8.3:1 of the production unit.

The more serious criticism of the BMC engine focused on the cylinder head and concerned the limitations the design placed on its tuning potential. The principal limitation was, justifiably, stated to be the porting of the cylinder head, which was similar to that of the early Austin Healey. The inlet ports were 'siamesed', allowing lower cost manufacturing but limiting the scope of tuning and so impairing high speed engine performance. Similarly, the two centre exhaust ports were siamesed, making exhaust tuning virtually impossible, though inlet port enlargement provided a partial problem on the induction side.

One technique which had been employed to improve the induction of the MGA's engine was to extend the inlet ports to the spark plug side of the cylinder head and fit a balancing pipe between the outer and inner cylinder inlet ports, boring out the original inlet ports as well. This had the effect of providing the opportunity of increasing the fuel charge from each of the carburettors and ensuring that there was sufficient mixture available for all four cylinders through the 1–3–4–2 firing sequence. The British tuning equipment manufacturer Westlake had devised a quite odd extension of this by fitting an additional pair of carburettors, the original pair fuelling the engine at low speed and the extra pair providing further fuel for high speed running. Balancing those carburettors would have been a nightmare, to say nothing of the awesome increase in fuel consumption which would result.

Despite the problems posed by the reviewing American press, the MGA was used in competition with considerable success, and many small tuning firms created tuning kits which improved the engine's performance. Two such firms were, of course, the supercharger makers Judson in America and Peco in Britain, both companies fitting a blower to the 'B' Series BMC engine to boost at between five and six pounds over atmosphere. The resulting improvement in performance was quite staggering for its time, the 0–60mph time with either installation reduced by a third to 11.2 seconds. Not too many 1,500cc-powered cars of the 1990s will turn in much better than that.

MG A ROADSTER

SPECIFICATIONS

List price	$2195
Wheelbase, in	94.0
Tread, front	47.4
rear	48.8
Tire size	5.60–15
Curb weight, lbs	2020
distribution, %	52/48
Test weight	2340
Engine	4-cly
Valves	pohv
Bore & stroke	2.875 x 3.5
Displacement, cu in	90.8
Compression ratio	8.30
Horsepower	68
peaking speed	5500
equivalent mph	93.6
Torque, ft/lbs	77.4
peaking speed	3500
equivalent mph	59.5
Mph per 1000 rpm	17.0
Mph at 2500 rpm	73.0
Gear ratios, (overall)	
4th	4.30
3rd	5.91
2nd	9.52
1st	15.65
R&T performance factor	39.1

PERFORMANCE

Top speed (avg)	95.1
best run	97.5
Max speeds in gears–	
3rd (6000)	74
2nd (6000)	46
1st (6000)	28
Shift points from–	
same as above	
Mileage range	28/32 mpg

ACCELERATION, Sec.

0–30 mph	4.6 secs
0–40 mph	6.8 secs
0–50 mph	10.2 secs
0–60 mph	14.5 secs
0–70 mph	19.9 secs
0–80 mph	30.4 secs
Standing ¼ mile–	
average	19.6 secs
best	19.3 secs

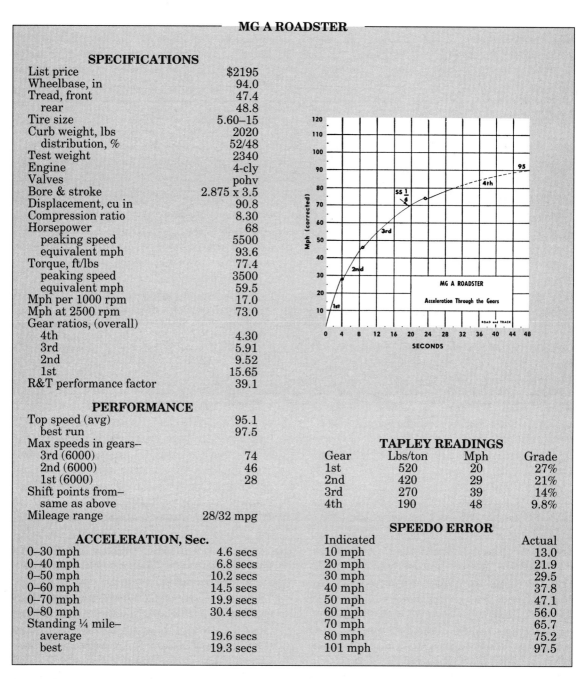

TAPLEY READINGS

Gear	Lbs/ton	Mph	Grade
1st	520	20	27%
2nd	420	29	21%
3rd	270	39	14%
4th	190	48	9.8%

SPEEDO ERROR

Indicated	Actual
10 mph	13.0
20 mph	21.9
30 mph	29.5
40 mph	37.8
50 mph	47.1
60 mph	56.0
70 mph	65.7
80 mph	75.2
101 mph	97.5

Road & Track *produced very comprehensive data tables in their road test reviews of sports cars. This is the one from the MGA 1500 test.*

MGAs for America. This batch of twenty-five cars was destined for Waco Motors of Miami, in Florida, who had sold them to a self-drive hire firm.

IMPRESSIONS FROM THE SOUTHERN HEMISPHERE

The spotlight of publicity in the post-war export drive embarked upon by the British motor industry seemed to focus almost entirely on successes in the North American market. However, there were deep loyalties to British cars in other English-speaking regions of the world, notably Australasia and Southern Africa, though not enough cars to satisfy demand in those markets. This had much to do with Britain's need for dollars to repay the massive war debt which had arisen from US military aid.

Even so, British vehicles found their way into what were traditional pre-war markets, such as Africa, the Indian sub-continent and Malaysia, as well as Australasia. It is interesting to note that British vehicles had a strong presence in all of these regions, as well as in the Arab Middle East at the time of the MGA's revelation to the markets of the world, so it made sense to exploit the potential of those markets as far as was possible (King Hussein of Jordan ran two 1500 MGAs among his other British sports cars). British trucks were predominant in East, West and South Africa, with British companies even assembling vehicles in those markets, whilst trucks were also sold to and assembled in India. Many Arab countries used British military trucks and utility cars were also being sold in numbers into Africa and India. Sports

The new MGA on show. Laying the vehicle on its side on a turntable display, gave a very good view of the interior space of the MGA and an excellent view of the seats and door line.

cars were a more specialist product and so sold on a more limited basis in terms of both numbers and markets. For example, they sold as well as availability allowed in South Africa, Australia and New Zealand, but in very limited numbers elsewhere.

On the road, the car was found to be surprisingly rugged in both Africa and Australasia, road testers being delighted with its handling and road-holding on the generally poorer surfaces common to those areas of the world. To the surprise of the Abingdon sales and service teams, dust filtration was not quite the problem to the 'B' Series engine that they had expected and so fuel consumption was not much below that of European and North American experience, being around 33–36 mpg (7.9–8.6l/100km) overall, comparing with around 28 miles per US gallon (8.4l/100km) – in other words about the same.

One tester criticized the location of the

MGA 1500

VEHICLE CONSTRUCTION
Rectangular-section steel-tube chassis with
fabricated scuttle 'bridge' and pressed steel body
structure with pressed steel panels

ENGINE

Crankcase/cylinder block	One piece cast iron
Cylinder head	Cast iron ohv
Cylinders	4
Compression ratio	8.3:1 standard (others optional)
Cooling system	Pressurized, thermo-syphon and pump
Bore and stroke	73.025 x 89mm
Engine capacity	1,489cc
Main bearings	Three shell-type
Valves	Single camshaft ohv pushrod/rocker
Fuel supply method and type	SU high pressure electric pump
Quoted max. power	68bhp @ 5,500rpm
Quoted max. torque	77.4lb/ft @ 3,500rpm

BRAKES

Type	Lockheed hydraulic drum, 2-leading shoe front
Size	10 x 1¾in front and rear

TRANSMISSION

Clutch type	Single dry plate Borg & Beck A6G
Gearbox ratios	R, 20.468:1; 1, 15.652:1; 2, 9.520:1; 3, 5.908:1; 4, 4.300:1 standard
Final drive ratio	Hypoid bevel 4.300:1 standard

SUSPENSION AND STEERING

Front suspension	Independent coil/piston dampers
Rear suspension	Semi-elliptic/piston dampers
Steering type	Rack and pinion, 2.66 turns
Wheel type and size	Ventilated disc 4J x 15in
Tyre size and rating	5.60 x 15in

VEHICLE DIMENSIONS (in/mm)

Overall length	156/3,962
Overall width	58/1,473
Wheelbase	94/2,388
Track	
front	47.5/1,206
rear	48.75/1,238
Overall height	50,1270

speedometer on the right-hand side of the dashboard, offering the comment that a navigator in competition would have great difficulty in seeing it. That was a curable fault, though, as it was possible to switch the speedometer and rev counter, but the over-flexible dashboard was less easily cured, so the manufacturer introduced bracing to eliminate the movement. The horn push was also criticized for not being in the hub of the steering wheel, which would have been a more logical place than on the dashboard. Also, the lack of two-speed windscreen wipers, even as an option, was commented upon – quite realistically when one considers the torrential downpours which occur in sub-tropical and tropical climates.

The greatly improved space for the car's occupants was applauded and the high door line helped keep out the dust on a long run. The seats were found to be comfortable on even the most tortuous surfaces and controls were considered generally to be responsive and light. All in all, the MGA was considered to be the best and potentially the most successful production MG yet built. History went on to prove that it was, with the best sales record, especially overseas, for any MG model hitherto.

4 Safety Faster, Record Breakers and a New MGA

The enthusiasm with which the MGA was received in the market place, and by the press, persuaded the British Motor Corporation that it had a winner on its hands. As a result, the decision was made to strengthen the competition activity by entering works cars in certain events and by supporting private entrants, as well as offering for sale stage tuning kits for the MGA engine and other competition accessories.

One of the earliest extras available was an oil cooler kit, an essential item for anyone planning to do anything more aggressive than hard road driving and even useful for the regular high speed, long-distance road driver. It consisted of a small oil radiator, mounted just ahead of the water radiator, and the piping which was essential to connect it to the oil filter and cylinder block for feed and return.

GOING SAFELY FASTER

There were several stages of tune available for the MGA, beginning with the fairly mild Stage One which featured the fitment of Type CC carburettor needles in the SUs and the polishing of the bottom face of the cylinder head as well as the inlet and exhaust ports. This was claimed to provide up to 7 bhp in addition to the quoted 68 bhp of the standard MGA engine as it left the Abingdon factory. Clearly, this was fine for the 'boy racer' type, but not much use to anyone else, except perhaps club level rally drivers.

Stage Two was more useful to the rally

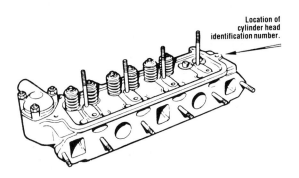

Location of cylinder head identification number.

From the Moss MGA parts catalogue comes this illustration of the 'B' Series BMC engine's cylinder head, showing the porting, two for inlet and three for exhaust, all on one side.

driver, with its improvement in mid-range acceleration and was intended to combine with Stage One to provide a similar overall power increase to that of Stage One, with an improvement of around 3 bhp in mid-range. It involved replacing the camshaft with a Riley One-Point-Five ignition distributor and camshaft (a dangerous name 'Riley', in MG circles) to give valve timing of 5/45/40/10, the inlet opening at 5 degrees before top dead centre and closing 45 degrees after bottom dead centre, whilst the exhaust valves opened at 40 degrees before bottom dead centre and closed 10 degrees after top dead centre. Valve lift was slightly reduced, from 0.357in to 0.322in, so the breathing restrictions of the cylinder head were slightly less of a problem and the overall useful power range was improved. The improvement in torque was not quoted. Riley had, of course, finally abandoned the famous twin-cam pushrod engine of the 1½-litre RME and 2½-litre Pathfinder models for 1956 (based on Percy Riley's original Riley Nine of thirty years before) with the introduction of the BMC 'B' Series-engined One-Point-Five and the six-cylinder Two-Point-Six.

A second step in Stage Two tune was the addition of 9:1 compression ratio pistons to replace the 8.3:1 standard fitment. These had flat tops instead of the concave tops of the originals and used fully floating gudgeon pins instead of the clamped type used in the standard pistons. This step was intended to restore some of the top-end performance which it was acknowledged was forfeit in the use of the Riley camshaft.

The next stage of tune for the original 1500 engine involved the polished ports and cylinder head face of Stage One, with the CC carburettor needles to improve fuel supply. But now pistons of 10:1 compression ratio were to be fitted, employing special heavy-duty connecting rods. As with the 9:1 pistons, fully-floating gudgeon pins were used, but the camshaft and distributor remained the standard fitments. The ignition setting was also changed from 7 degrees to 2 degrees before top dead centre. Harder spark plugs were recommended and it was essential to use 100 Octane fuel. The effect of all this was to increase the maximum power to 86 bhp at 6,000rpm. Finally, 1¾-in SU carburettors, with KW needles, on a special inlet manifold, could be fitted to improve the fuelling, and so acceleration, of this conversion.

NON-FACTORY TUNING OPTIONS

The one thing which the factory did not do that really would have benefitted the MGA engine more than any other conversion was to offer an alternative to the standard BMC 'B' Series cylinder head. So it was left to others to investigate and develop improvements in that area. One such improvement came from H.R.G. (the H.R.G. car was an H.R. Godfrey improvement of the pre-war Frazer Nash cars, but was discontinued almost as soon as the MGA was announced to the world), a company with much experience of engine development and special tuning.

The H.R.G. cylinder head was offered to the market place by V.W. Derrington of Kingston upon Thames, one of the longest established purveyors of tuning equipment for MG sports cars in the business, but sadly no longer providing their particular selection of car bits for the enthusiast. Their aluminium alloy cylinder head with cross-flow porting, specially designed for the 'B' Series BMC engine, was proven to be capable of increasing power and torque output by up to 25 per cent with the quite standard carburation of two 1½in SUs.

Of course, while it was perfectly feasible to fit only the Derrington H.R.G. cylinder head and use the standard MGA exhaust system, standard 8.3:1 compression ratio and original SU carburettors, one of the values of using the H.R.G. head was the fact that it could be used in conjunction with other tuning components to make significant performance improvements and all at no greater risk to the basic engine than the factory tuning kits might inflict. The cost, too, was little different.

Using the H.R.G. cylinder head with other tuning components, such as higher compression pistons (9.2:1 ratio) and a pair of twin-choke Weber carburettors, it was possible to raise the power output to over 108 bhp and torque to well over 100lb/ft (150kg/m). The basic engine was still not over-stressed, although in this last configuration, the engine speed was increased to 6,000rpm from the factory standard 5,750rpm of the production MGA engine. Some also used this Derrington tuning combination with high performance, high lift camshafts as they became available.

This extract from the Derrington catalogue gives quite a lot of information about the benefits of the HRG/Derrington cylinder head, including two pictures of the head, showing the cross-flow porting, with four inlets instead of two. The prices make interesting reading, too.

The H.R.G.head has been extremely successful when used for racing and provided the face has not been weakened by over machining,the correct gasket used,stout washers under the head nuts,and not tightened over 40 lbs ft.the head should give long and reliable service.

It is of course most valuable for normal use on the road owing to the greatly increased torque from 1,000 R.P.M upwards and a similar increase of power which has not even reached its peak at 6,000 R.P.M.and is limited only by the valve bounce,or other factors. A car fitted with the H.R.G.head is most flexible and careful fuel consumption tests have shown an improvement of at least 10% on the same carburetters,when suitably set for road use. The H.R.G.head gives such an increase of power and torque that a lower axle ratio can beneficially be used. Engine revolutions are lowered in relation to road speeds,reducing wear and improving fuel consumption,various alternative ratios being available. Bearing reliability can be improved by the fitting of an oil radiator supplied as a complete kit with flexible high pressure pipes and connections. Under racing and high speed conditions in air temperature over 80F the oil cooler reduces the working temperature of the oil by 20° C improving bearing reliability and lowering oil consumption.

All H.R.G.cylinder heads are supplied complete with valves ground in and spring assemblies fitted ready for use. The kit of parts supplied with the cylinder head includes all necessary studs and nuts,clamping bars for the exhaust manifold,universal jointed sparking plug spanner and tommy bar,throttle control bracket,competition cylinder head and port gaskets.

 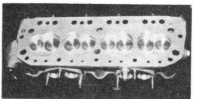

DERRINGTON/H.R.G.CYLINDER HEAD. Price list	£. s. d.	new US$. rate
Mk.IV Head kit complete with valves & springs,assembled	79 0 0	189.60
Machining face for higher C/R .025"(at time of ordering)	1 10 0	3.60
" " " " " .040"(")	2 10 0	6.00
Race preparation,special valves,guides,springs and porting	16 0 0	38.40
Inlet pipe,balanced for H.4,HS.4 or H6.S.U. carburetters	10 10 0	25.20
S.U.needles for H.4 4/3d each,50cts, for H.6. S.U. carbs. each	7 6	.90
Inlet pipe with twin H.6 S.U carburetters,linkages,fuel pipe	36 10 0	87.60
Inlet assy complete with 40 DCOE WEBERS having suitable jet & choke settings,throttle adaptor & fuel pipe lin	60 0 0	144.00
Assembly as above, but with 45 DCOE WEBERS	66 0 0	158.40
9-1 pistons,flat top for 1496 c/c C/W rings & pins, per set		
9-1 " " " 1588 c/c " " " " " "	9 10 0	22.80
Water valve adaptor,for re-positioning water valve away from head	17 6	1.80
Head kits,packing in strong hardboard box & carriage, INLAND	1 0 0	
" " " " " " postage,(2 parcels)INLAND	1 5 0	
U.S.A & CANADA in two separate parcels		14.00

For posting overseas,the cylinder head weighing 21 lbs is boxed in one parcel,the valves being numbered for correct assembly and included with all the other parts in a separate parcel,this method of despatch avoiding expensive shipping charges.

SUPERCHARGING THE MGA

A sports car enthusiast named Vernon Farthing, from Liverpool, was the managing director of a company known as the Performance Equipment Company, usually abbreviated to 'Peco'. They produced an exhaust attachment which claimed to 'boost' the exhaust system by assisting the extraction of exhaust gases from the system, so improving gas flow and fuel consumption. They also sold their own brand of extractor exhaust system, of which the booster was a part, with a specially designed straight-through silencer which had a resonating chamber built in. Vernon Farthing was reputed to be an expert in gas flow and his exhaust products certainly sold well, to MG owners as well as other motorists.

Improving the performance of the MGA

beyond exhaust gas extraction was Mr Farthing's self-set task in this case and he decided that a low-pressure supercharger would provide the solution. He reasoned that his modifications would have an added attraction to the MG owner if they could be reversed without high cost or detriment to the car, particularly in the area of its resale value. So the Peco supercharger and exhaust system were very carefully designed to ensure that they could be removed and the original induction and exhaust system restored with no trace of the blower having been fitted in the first place.

The installation featured an inlet manifold which bolted directly in place of the original twin-carburettor manifold, to carry the Roots-type blower with its single SU carburettor. The supercharger's carburettor had a special needle designed by Peco and the whole assembly was fitted with the minimum of problems, the supercharger requiring no additional space to house it than the original induction system needed. Therefore, there was no need to make any bodywork modifications. Lubrication for the supercharger was drawn from the dipstick hole via a removable flexible pipe, which allowed the continuing use of the dipstick to check levels by simply lifting out the pipe and replacing it after the oil check was complete.

Normal boost pressure was set at between 5 and 6lb/in^2 (0.35 and 0.42kg/cm^2) and drive to the supercharger was by means of a belt from the crankshaft. Belt adjustment needed some care to ensure proper alignment, but once this was done, belt life was expected to be around 20,000 miles (32,000km). With the exhaust system replaced almost bolt-for-bolt, the car was ready for the road. Supercharger noise was apparent, but not obtrusive and the exhaust had a little more 'bark' than on the original car, but again, it was not offensive. There were no other modifications to carry out on the car, though it seems the Peco test car did have a heavier duty clutch, to

allow more for enthusiastic road testers than to meet any technical need.

Performance improvement from this blower installation was noteworthy, not least because the basic engine was totally unmodified, retaining its 8.3:1 compression ratio, valves, guides, springs and cylinder head, though the ports were almost certainly polished for optimum results. One critical point, however, was that the driver was warned not to exceed 5,800rpm, as much as anything else because the unmodified state of the engine meant there was a risk of severe overheating, with valve bounce occurring at higher engine speeds while there was still mixture in the combustion chambers. A yellow warning light was even clipped to the dashboard to remind the driver when he reached 5,800rpm, so strong was the maker's insistence on the limit.

Engine rev limits apart, the Peco supercharged MGA was quite a performer, taking some two and a half seconds off the 0–60mph time, bringing it down to almost exactly thirteen seconds – a much more respectable time. More than a second was trimmed from the standing quarter mile time and speeds through the gears were similarly improved. At the same time, the car was found to be remarkably docile, when required, something one would not expect of a supercharged car – and certainly not of a supercharged MG with the pre-war blown cars in mind. The other astonishing feature of this car's performance was the fuel consumption. Peco's claim was for 30mpg (9.4l/100km), almost one mile per gallon better than the standard car's average, and this was proved in road tests.

So, out of all this, for around £100 at the time, the MGA owner could enjoy a marked improvement in the performance of his car, a slight improvement in fuel consumption arising from the more efficient combustion of less mixture and a car which could quite quickly be restored to standard specification without trace of there having been a supercharger in place at all. There was, and probably still is, a certain fear associated with the disposal of supercharged cars, the general impression being that they have been thrashed unmercifully (which may be equally true of a car in naturally aspirated state), so here the car could be sold in completely factory standard form as a used sports car. Also, the seller could retain his blower and Peco exhaust system for transfer to another car, though the exhaust would, of course, only transfer to another MGA.

MGS TO THE MILLE MIGLIA – AGAIN

The last but one Mille Miglia was run on 29 April 1956 and, for the first time in many a long year there were MGs in the list of starters, of which that year there were 365. Not since the great race of 1933, when three

K3 Magnettes were entered, driven by Earl Howe/H.C. Hamilton, Sir Henry Birkin/ Bernard Rubin (these two being ex-'Bentley Boys') and Captain George Eyston/Count Giovanni Lurani. Back then, the MG team won the Gran Premio Brescia Team Prize, despite the fact that the Birkin/ Rubin car went out at Siena. The other two performed better than any British car had ever performed, either before or since, taking the first two places in their class, the Howe/Hamilton car following the Eyston/ Lurani Magnette by just a minute and a half.

For the 1956 Mille Miglia there were again three MGs entered, this time MGAs. Two cars were works entries, one driven by well known rally driver Nancy Mitchell, passengered (but not co-driven) by Pat Faichney, and the other by P. Scott-Russell and T. Haigh. The third car was an Italian private entry and the event was one of the wettest Mille Miglias on record. To finish at all was the aim, the prospect of a class

Nancy Mitchell and Pat Faichney took this MGA on the 1956 Mille Miglia. Miss Mitchell drove the whole distance and, despite never having driven in a Mille Miglia, nor having driven the course of the 1956 event, she finished in seventy-fourth place overall, just two places behind the other works car, and fifth in her class.

position being thought too remote to pin hopes on. In MG team terms, it was actually a pretty casual affair, Nancy Mitchell driving the whole distance in her car, her passenger simply being there for the companionship. Interestingly, Nancy Mitchell hadn't even driven the course before the event, preferring to rely on her rally-developed reflexes to guide her through new and interesting terrain.

The works MGAs were not extensively tuned racing cars, though they were fitted with 25-gallon (115-litre) fuel tanks, aero screens instead of the full-width standard screen, a Lucas 'Flamethrower' spotlamp, high final drive ratio and more powerful horns. The passenger had a rear view mirror on the near side of the car, so as to see oncoming fast cars coming up from behind. The standard bumpers were removed and the cars were prepared by factory mechanics. But apart from being very carefully put together, the car's specifications were to catalogue standard and they were entered in the 'Sports Car of Limited Price' Class.

Such were the rigours of this race that only 182 of the 365 starters finished the event. After the stupendous Moss/Jenkinson victory for Mercédès-Benz in 1955, the German factory cars were almost also-rans in this 1956 race. Victory this time went to Eugenio Castellotti's Ferrari, followed into second place by another Ferrari crewed by Peter Collins/Louis Klemantaski and three more behind them to give Ferrari the first five places. Mercédès-Benz took the next three.

Of the two MGAs to finish, the Scott-Russell/Haigh car was third in its class and seventy-second overall, whilst Nancy Mitchell was just a couple of places behind, despite having had no practice or 'dry run' prior to the race. So she was seventy-fourth overall and fifth in her class. In addition to that, she and Pat Faichney were given a surprise award as the first all-female crew to finish. Their race time of a little over fifteen

hours gave them a speed of over 60mph (195km/h) average, the Scott-Russell/Haig car's time being fifteen hours, two minutes and seventeen seconds; an average speed of over 65mph (105km/h). Although 1500cc MGAs took part in a lot of other races during its relatively short life, the 1956 Mille Miglia must rank as the most important race since the EX182s' success in the 1955 Le Mans 24 Hours, for this race truly put the stamp of durability and reliability on the MGA.

THE RECORD BREAKERS

Speed records were a special part of the MG story from the time of the 'M' Type Midget, two of the most famous being the 'Magic Midget' (EX127, the first 750cc car to exceed 120mph (195km/h)) and Captain George Eyston's EX135, which later passed into the hands of Major A.T.G. 'Goldie' Gardner, who had the car re-bodied to become one of the most elegant (and successful) record cars ever built. Two particular MG record breakers associated with the MGA were EX179 and EX181, both of which established new International Class F records and did much to further the reputation and sales of the MGA.

EX179 was built in 1953/4 for Captain George Eyston's successful run at eight Class F records and was basically the proving car for Syd Enever's MGA chassis design, but by 1956 it was destined to undertake another proving task in the quest to develop the MGA. Now, it was to run with an engine that was ultimately to be fitted to the MGA chassis and become a new model, the MGA Twin-Cam. But before that, fifteen new international records were to be established.

During the summer of 1956 there was quite a flurry of record breaking. It began with a 750cc Abarth, bodied by Bertone and run at Monza to break the International Class H 3,000-Kilometre, 24-Hour and 4,000-Kilometre records. Then came Piero

This picture shows the chassis of EX179, with its body frame mounted, but no panels. This is clearly an early shot of the car, as it is still left-hand drive and fitted with the TF1500–type XPEG engine.

Taruffi, with a supercharged Maserati-engined special of his own making, to take the 100-Miles, 200-Kilometres and One-Hour records in Class E. But his top speed of 140.29mph (225.87km/h) was soon eclipsed by Britons John Lockett and Ken Miles, driving EX179 at Bonneville Salt Flats in Utah, when the Ten-Mile Flying Start Record was elevated to an amazing 170.15mph (273.94km/h).

The body design of EX179 bore a striking resemblance to that of Reid Railton's body built for 'Goldie' Gardner on EX135 as long ago as 1939. But why not, when EX135 had already proved the streamlined shape with its outstanding achievements. The driving seat in EX179 was offset to the right and the car was slightly smaller and lower than EX135. It was powered by a version of the twin-cam engine which had been installed into the EX182 car driven at the RAC Ulster Tourist Trophy Race the year before by John Lockett and Ron Flockhart, still at this time running at 1500cc capacity. The records they achieved speak for themselves, as Lockett and Miles took fifteen international records from the 50-Kilometre through to the Class F Twelve-Hour record at 141.71mph (228.15km/h). And as if that weren't enough, they also established forty-eight national US records as well.

After EX179's tremendous run in that summer of 1956, the decision was made to produce a twin-cam version of the MGA for sale to the public. But while that was on the drawing-board, another record breaker was also in hand, this one to test the twin-cam engine design to the limit. The engine was to be a supercharged version of the unit already developed and the chassis was to be a totally

Here, EX179 stands on the salt flats with Ken Miles and Johnny Lockett alongside it, presumably before their record run in 1956 (as the car looks clean and unblemished). With the twin-cam engine, it exceeded 170mph (275km/h), though to accommodate the revised engine installation, the steering column had to be moved to the right hand side from the left.

new design largely based on the research carried out for the World Land Speed Record by John Cobb's team some years earlier.

The MGA was now well and truly established in the market place and sales were better than anything anyone at Abingdon ever dared hope for. But there had been comments from certain reviewers and from

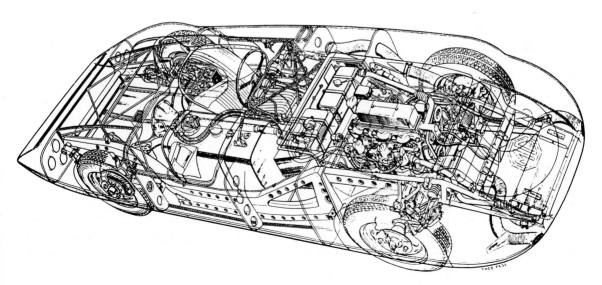

This Theo Page cutaway drawing of EX179, from the pages of Autosport, *clearly shows the chassis form, though again this is the car in its original form with the XPEG engine.*

dealers in North America that the car was a little underpowered in standard form and that many people did not want to either incur the cost or go to the trouble of having their car speed-tuned. Apart from any other reason, they did not want the extra insurance costs which came with modified cars (the insurance companies were at it even then!). They simply wanted more power from the standard production model MGA. So the twin-cam engine was put into the production plan, but not before it was proved reliable and capable of taking far more punishment than it ever would on the road.

EX181 LEADS TO THE TWIN-CAM

EX181 was to be the means of punishing that twin-cam engine beyond any normal limits, for apart from any normal high-speed running stresses that it might be subjected to, the engine in EX181, though based on the existing BMC 'B' series engine of the MGA, was to be supercharged. Eddie Maher, Chief Experimental Engineer at BMC's Morris Engines Branch in Coventry (under the nominal guidance of his boss, Chief Development Engineer J. Thompson), took up the challenge of creating a record-breaking variation

The twin-cam engine had its pilot record run in EX179, but then it was developed further, and supercharged, for installation in EX181, with sights set on four miles a minute.

E. J. Maher CEng MIMechE ARAeS (1910–76)

'Eddie' Maher started his higher education in his native Ireland on the path of civil engineering. However, his direction changed when he saw an early Riley 'procession' in the 1929 Irish Grand Prix. Captain George Eyston (a name linked very closely to MG 'Magic') finished fourth overall to win the 1,100cc Class in a race of just under 270 miles (435km). Eyston was followed into second to sixth places in Class by Victor Gillow, Jack Dunfee, Cyril Whitcroft, Jack Boal and Kaye Don, all driving Rileys. Having seen Kenneth Peacock drive a Riley to win the 1,100cc Class in the previous year's Ulster Tourist Trophy Race, Eddie Maher decided he wanted to be associated with and involved in that kind of success, so did no more than apply for an apprenticeship with Riley, being admitted to that company in the summer of 1929.

While studying for Institution of Mechanical Engineers examinations, Eddie decided he liked aeroplanes and so began to study Aeronautical Engineering, too. Upon completion of his apprenticeship, he moved into the Competitions Department of Riley (Coventry) Limited – quite an accolade for a young man just out of indentures. Remaining with the Competition Department of Riley's until the demise of the company and its entry into the Nuffield empire, he transferred to development engineering and then came the Second World War. Aero engine induction systems quickly became Eddie's speciality during the war years and it was he who solved many fuel supply problems connected with the Rolls-Royce Merlin engine.

When Riley moved to Abingdon (to join MG), Eddie Maher stayed in Coventry, where his services were in demand as a development engineer at the Morris Engines Branch at Courthouse Green in Coventry. He was very much involved at the leading edge of engine development for the whole of the Nuffield and later British Motor Corporation groups of companies, which included the MGA Twin-Cam engine and its precursors used in the prototype EX182 cars and the record-breaker EX181. It was Eddie Maher's team which was selected to develop the engine destined to become the production Twin-Cam MGA power unit and he who coaxed it into production from the drawing board.

Retiring in 1975, Eddie Maher had led a full and active life, having produced the engine which came so close to winning at Le Mans in 1934, but having also, directly out of that experience, created the engine which propelled a 1½-litre engined car to four miles a minute for the first time. Sadly, he died a year later, before having the chance to enjoy his retirement.

of the twin-cam unit which had been run in the 1955 Tourist Trophy Race and which was now to be the next generation of the MGA. It was hardly surprising that Eddie Maher, former Chief Development Engineer of Riley (Coventry) Limited in the days before that company became a part of the Nuffield empire, produced a cylinder head design which followed closely the concepts of Percy Riley's immortal Nine engine of the 1920s and 1930s.

Like the Riley Nine (and the 1½-litre which followed it) this new MG engine had hemispherical combustion chambers, valves operating at 80 degrees from each other and 50 degrees from the horizontal plane (the pre-war Riley valve angles were 90 and 45 degrees), but with duplex chain drive rather than gear drive (chains made less noise and were adjustable. Valves were operated by the chain-drive camshafts via bucket tappets and two 2¹/₁₆ SU carburettors fed the mixture to the Shorrock eccentric-vane supercharger which provided an induction pressure of 2.2 atmospheres. Methanol-based fuel was to be used to wring out some 295bhp at 7,300rpm. That was a pretty phenomenal power output for a four cylinder engine based on a production unit (the bore and stroke remained the same as in the 1,489cc MGA engine) and compares remarkably well with what hitherto had been the most powerful 1,500cc engine ever, the Alfa Romeo 158 'Alfetta' Grand Prix engine. The Italian unit produced a massive 425bhp in its final form, but that was as a two-stage supercharged all-alloy eight-cylinder pure racing engine on which large blocks of development cash had been invested.

The chassis of EX181 was a total departure for MG, in that it was the first mid-engined MG, again borrowing an idea from John Cobb's 'Thunderbolt', with the 'pilot' sitting at the front of the car. Auto-Union had used this concept for their pre-Second World War Grand Prix cars with great success and the biggest unraced threat to early post-war Grand Prix racing, the Alfa Romeo 512 embodied the same concepts. EX181's frame consisted of two large-diameter round longitudinal tubes in ladder form sweeping up and over the rear axle, ending at the front with quite orthodox independent front suspension. The mid-located engine had a four-speed synchromesh gearbox which connected, via a 6in (152mm) long propeller shaft to the differential.

The independent rear suspension of the car used a de Dion tube and splayed quarter-elliptic leaf springs, assisted by Armstrong piston-type shock absorbers. Rigid trailing links, welded at their outer ends to the hub carriers, positioned the rear wheels longitudinally. With a very narrow track of only 2ft 6¾in (781mm), the drive shafts from the differential were very short and ran from the inboard-mounted disc brakes (there were no front brakes) to the hubs by Hardy Spicer universal joints. To support the body, two large frame hoops were welded to the chassis, so endowing it with rollover protection in the process of their installation. Bodywork was of 18 gauge hyduminium alloy, all-welded, with the nose section on a separate subframe and the tail section a

frameless structure. Weight distribution was 51.5 per cent front and 48.5 per cent rear, the dry weight of the car being 1,655lb (750kg).

By August 1957 EX181 was finally ready for its attempt on a number of International Class F records, with the positive aim of raising the new record to over 240mph (385km/h). The little blue projectile had sailed from Southampton on the Queen Mary (nothing but the best!) and the stage was set for Stirling Moss to make his attempt on Wednesday 21 August. The weather had something to say about that, however, and rain storms caused the postponement of the run to the following Friday. American racing driver Phil Hill had done the preliminaries and Moss climbed aboard just before dusk to make his official run.

Five International Class F records fell to Stirling Moss and MG's EX181 on the evening of Friday 23 August 1957. All were Flying Start records, beginning with the One-Kilometre at the astonishing speed of 245.64mph (395.48km/h). The One-Mile record fell at 245.11mph (394.63km/h), the Five-Kilometre going down at 243.08mph (391.48km/h), whilst the new Five-Mile record went to Moss at 235.69mph (379.46 km/h). Finally, the new Ten-Kilometre record was set at 224.7mph (361.8km/h). This meant that Stirling Moss had broken all five of 'Goldie' Gardner's former records, each by more than 40mph (65km/h)! With that tremendous record success behind the MG team, the die was now cast. Soon, there would be a twin-cam variant of the MGA available to the world's public.

THE TWIN-CAM MGA TAKES THE STAGE

From the very beginning of the MGA's life, there was a body of opinion that said the car needed more power than was available in the

EX181, seen here on its run with Stirling Moss at the wheel, was much more of a 'tear-drop' shape in profile. Moss achieved the target of four miles a minute with five mph to spare, but two years later, in 1959, American racing ace Phil Hill took the car to 254mph (409km/h) – nearly four and a quarter miles per minute on a 1,500cc engine.

standard pushrod-engined 1,500cc version. The risk of heavy insurance penalties on modified engines certainly dissuaded many a British buyer from going down the road of special tuning kits, even though they might be factory approved, because such a step would mean that they had modified the car from catalogue standard. Modifying and 'tweaking' is a precarious business in any event and if the public could buy a more powerful version of their favourite sports car, the temptation to tamper with the standard engine might be avoided. And then there was the point that, with the Twin-Cam, Abingdon could enjoy all of the available profit while offering a standard catalogue model.

So it was that the new MGA Twin-Cam was announced to the public in the summer of 1958. From the outside, it looked virtually identical to the pushrod-engined version, which it was not intended to supersede, but rather to be offered as an up-market sibling. While the body and exterior trim were the same in principle, there were a few little detail variations that the discerning 'MGA spotter' would identify. For example, on the outside, it had centre-lock disc wheels with larger tyres (5.90 x 15 instead of 5.60 x 15), a 'Twin Cam' logo behind the bonnet vents and inside, a vinyl-covered dashboard and deluxe seats.

Under the skin, of course, the Twin-Cam

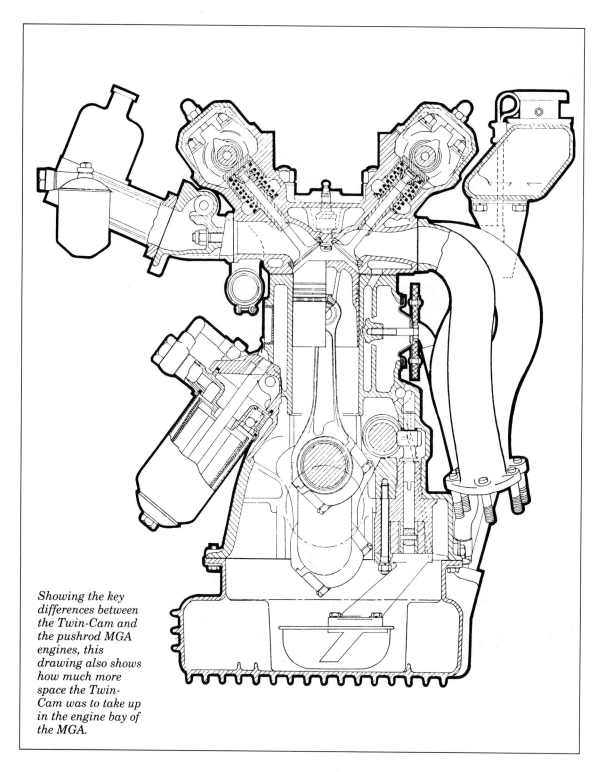

Showing the key differences between the Twin-Cam and the pushrod MGA engines, this drawing also shows how much more space the Twin-Cam was to take up in the engine bay of the MGA.

The MGA Twin-Cam Roadster as it first appeared. This is clearly a prototype, as it does not yet display any of the distinctive 'Twin-Cam' badging behind the scuttle vent badge. But it does have the four-peg drive centre-lock disc road wheels.

was significantly different in several areas, yet remarkably the same in others. The chassis was basically the same, except that the car now had disc brakes all round, the steering rack mounting was different and the brake lines were modified to accommodate the disc brakes. The engine, of course, was different, in that it used the 'B' Series BMC cylinder block, but now was of 1,588cc capacity (the bore was enlarged to 75.4mm) and, of course, had the twin-cam alloy cylinder head. Compression ratio of the engine was now up to 9.9:1, with domed pistons running on fully floating gudgeon pins, instead of the earlier clamped type, and there were a few minor variations in the chassis detail. The rear axle assembly was different, too, with pin-drive hubs. Here it was then, the first-ever production MG to be offered for sale with a Twin-Cam engine.

5   The Twin-Cam Sets New Standards

Here at last was the 100mph-plus MGA that the market had wanted for some time. The original MGA had been an excellent seller and from Abingdon's point of view had been an enormous success. Almost 31,000 cars had been sold by the end of 1957 and another 14,800-plus would sell by the end of 1958, bringing the total to over 45,000 cars in a little over three years. The MG Car Company and the British Motor Corporation had just cause to be pleased with themselves, though they could not, and did not, rest on their laurels. They had reacted to the comments of the market place and the press and read in advance the signs of a slight decline in sales. The 1958 sales figure was almost 2,500 (over 9 per cent) below the 1957 figure and while that figure would certainly have been influenced by the introduction of the Twin-Cam, the signs of a downturn were there and the makers' reading of them was timely.

THE TWIN-CAM IS LAUNCHED

First press news of the MGA 1600 Twin-Cam reached the public in the middle of 1958. The press corps was invited to an introduction staged at the War Department's Fighting Vehicles Research and Development Establishment at Chobham in Surrey, where there was an opportunity to

The Twin-Cam's introduction came with a test day at the military vehicle development centre at Chobham. Outwardly, the car looks little different from the 1500, other than the immediate giveaway of the new car's centre-lock disc wheels.

MGA Twin-Cam

VEHICLE CONSTRUCTION	
Rectangular-section steel-tube chassis with fabricated scuttle 'bridge' and pressed steel body structure with pressed steel panels	

ENGINE

Crankcase/cylinder block	One piece cast iron
Cylinder head	Aluminium alloy ohc
Cylinders	4
Compression ratio	9.9:1 standard
Cooling system	Pressurized, thermo-syphon and pump
Bore and stroke	75.41 x 89mm
Engine capacity	1,588cc
Main bearings	Three shell-type
Valves	Twin overhead cam, chain driven
Fuel supply method and type	SU high pressure electric pump
Quoted max. power	108bhp @ 6,700rpm
Quoted max. torque	105lb/ft @ 4,500rpm

BRAKES

Type	Dunlop disc brakes front and rear with mechanical handshake linkage
Size	11in

TRANSMISSION

Clutch type	Single dry plate Borg & Beck 8ARG

Gearbox ratios	R, 20.468:1;
	1, 15.652:1;
	2, 9.520:1;
	3, 5.908:1;
	4, 4.300:1; standard
	R, 13.75:1;
	1, 10,51:1;
	2, 6.966:1;
	3, 5.449: 1;
Final drive ratio	4, 4.300:1 optional
	4.300:1 (4.55:1 optional)

SUSPENSION AND STEERING

Front suspension	Independent coil/piston dampers
Rear suspension	Semi-eliptic/piston dampers
Steering type	Rack and pinion, 2.66 turns
Wheel type and size	Ventilated disc 4J x 15in
Tyre size and rating	5.90 x 15in Dunlop Roadspeed

VEHICLE DIMENSIONS (in/mm)

Overall length	156/3,962
Overall width	58/1,473
Wheelbase	94/2,388
Track	
front	47.91/1,216
rear	48.875/1,241
Overall height	50/1,270

---

try out the performance of this new MG without the interruption of other traffic. They were not disappointed.

Early impressions of the MGA Twin-Cam were that nothing of the original car's road-holding and general handling had been lost in the creation of this new model. Indeed, the extra power was greatly appreciated, as it provided the driver with the opportunity to better enjoy the responsiveness and sensitivity of the original design. Cornering could now be taken closer to the car's design limits. Acceleration was much improved, with a whole two seconds taken off the 0–60mph time. But certain, relatively minor though quite important, specification changes had been made to accommodate this improvement in performance.

The design team at Abingdon had felt a need to improve the car's grip of the road so, to provide for the larger tyre section (low-aspect ratio tyres were still a thing of the future in 1958) a minor modification to the steering arms was incorporated, which allowed also for the slightly longer power unit and accommodated the revisions in brake specification.

THE METAMORPHOSIS OF THE TWIN-CAM

With the proving experience of the twin-cam-engined EX182 car competing in the 1955 RAC Tourist Trophy Race, it would have been very easy for MG simply to have fitted a twin-cam engine with no chassis modifications whatever. The resulting product would have been a better car than the pushrod-engined 1500, its braking and handling would have been no worse than many other sports cars being offered at the time and it would have kept the price down. But that was not the way things were done at Abingdon. 'Safety Fast' remained the motto of the MG factory.

The steering rack was similar to that used on the original 1500cc pushrod-engined MGA, but was, as has been said, moved forward to allow for the installation of the longer twin-cam power unit. The steering arms, linking the rack to the front wheels, were beefed up a little to cope with the increased workload of a car with better performance, bigger tyres and better brakes. The higher tyre specification meant an improvement of around 12in² (75cm²) in tyre surface contact area, which helped to make the car slightly more sure-footed towards the top end of its performance envelope, and also improve the car's grip under heavy braking and its stability at high speeds.

Because the Twin-Cam had been endowed with an almost 20mph (30km/h) increase in maximum road speed, the Abingdon design team wanted to leave nothing to chance and so decided, in addition to the changes to tyres, to make a drastic improvement in the car's braking ability. While the drum brakes of the original MGA had been highly praised by all who drove the car, the increase of 40bhp and an increase of almost 30lb/ft in torque suggested that drum brakes might be pushed close to their safe limit in the new car, so disc brakes were fitted.

While Girling disc brakes had been used in EX181 during its record runs at Bonneville, Dunlop was chosen to provide the stopping equipment of this new MGA and 10¾in discs were fitted to the front and rear of the Twin-Cam, with mechanical actuation of the rear callipers for the handbrake. The handbrake was to prove the Twin-Cam's Achilles heel, as nobody had yet successfully managed to create a mechanical linkage which could effectively clamp brake pads on to a disc, rather than expand shoes into a drum. Many manufacturers (Porsche being among the first) returned to a drum-type handbrake via the expedient of having a small drum cast integrally with the rear brake discs, to provide the means for a separate handbrake mechanism to work.

Dunlop road wheels had been a standard fitment to MGAs from the very first and were also a standard fitment to this new car, though this time they were of centre-lock disc type, rather than the four stud type used on the earlier model. This use of centre-lock disc wheels on the Twin-Cam offered lower weight than centre-lock wire wheels, while retaining the advantage of one-nut wheel removal. It also allowed the manufacturer to hold down production costs as disc wheels still cost less to make than wires, and the cost of the centre-lock hub added very little over the cost of a four-stud assembly. An incidental benefit of these new wheels was that they demanded much less maintenance and were, in fact, a great deal stronger than conventional wire wheels, apart from which they actually suited the line of the car better.

THE TWIN-CAM'S POWERHOUSE

The very first time a twin-cam engine was considered for the MGA, it may be remembered that two designs were put on the drawing-board, one at Coventry under the supervision of Eddie Maher with his Morris

Behind the disc wheels of the Twin-Cam hid Dunlop disc brakes. The Twin-Cam MGA was only the second production small sports car in Britain to be fitted with disc brakes as standard equipment.

Engines design team and the other at the Austin plant at Longbridge. The Longbridge team was headed by a man named Bill Appleby, whose competition engine experience had been largely acquired under the guidance of Murray Jamieson, the man who designed the supercharger for Raymond Mays' pre-war English Racing Automobiles voiturette, as well as the twin-cam 750cc engine which so successfully powered Austin's racing single-seater of the late 1930s.

Appleby's engine design used the 'clean-sheet-of-paper' approach, though he would almost certainly have used much of the experience he gained from the Austin twin-cam in the concept. One such engine saw the light of day at the 1955 TT, though it was given scant attention at the time and certainly wasn't pushed into the limelight, because no decision at that point had been made as to which engine would go into production. On the bench, the Longbridge twin-cam performed well and seemed to offer considerable promise as a candidate to power the new version of the MGA when it came.

This is the other twin-cam engine developed for the MGA – the Appleby-designed unit developed at Longbridge. Here, it is in one of the EX182 cars, but was abandoned in favour of the Coventry developed engine based on the 'B' Series BMC unit, on the grounds of cost.

When the two engine designs were presented for the Longbridge-based BMC Board's decision, apart from the obvious question of how either type could be expected to perform, one consideration which was almost certain to over-ride nearly anything else would be the matter of production costing and the ultimate effect of that costing on the selling price of the finished product. The 'clean-sheet-of-paper' approach of the Appleby design was a major factor in the decision not to adopt it as the production unit for the twin-cam MGA. The Coventry design's use of a large range of existing components in its construction was what won it the day.

While the engine which powered the record-breaking EX181 was a 1,500cc unit, Appendix J of the International Sporting Code now allowed a 1,600cc capacity limit and so, apart from the advantage of that to the MGA, insurance groupings were also moving upwards to accommodate 1,600cc-engined cars, and the British motor industry at large was reviewing engine sizes for production cars. As a consequence, BMC had already decided to increase the capacity of

A production Twin-Cam engine on the bench . . .

the 'B' Series engine to 1,588cc, by the simple expedient of increasing the bore.

For the twin-cam MGA design team, the decision to increase the 'B' Series to a 1,588cc unit was a considerable boon, because the extraction of the required extra horsepower and torque would be a slightly less stressful task. It had already been decided that Eddie Maher's engine would use the cylinder block/crankcase of the existing standard power unit. The use of chain drive for the camshafts, from a sprocket behind the intermediate timing gear in the original 'B' Series crankcase/cylinder block, provided a potentially quieter operation of camshaft drive than by gear train, though gears were used in the standard production pushrod 'B' Series engine that powered the various family cars and light commercials produced by the British Motor Corporation companies.

But chain-driven camshafts in the Twin-Cam also meant lower manufacturing costs.

The single camshaft of the pushrod design was replaced by a jackshaft which drove the ignition distributor at its front end, the Hobourn-Eaton oil pump fitted to the new engine at its centre and the rev counter at the rear end. The Twin-Cam also had 9.9:1 high-crown pistons in lieu of the standard (though 8.3:1 compression ratio was available) and, to keep all that clean, a large full-flow oil filter was fitted. Access to the camshafts was easy: five studs on each cam cover held them down, three down the centre-line of each and two more on the front flange where the faces of the cam boxes met the top face of the front-mounted timing cover.

The aluminium alloy cylinder head of the Twin-Cam was of cross-flow design, with classic Riley-type hemispherical combustion

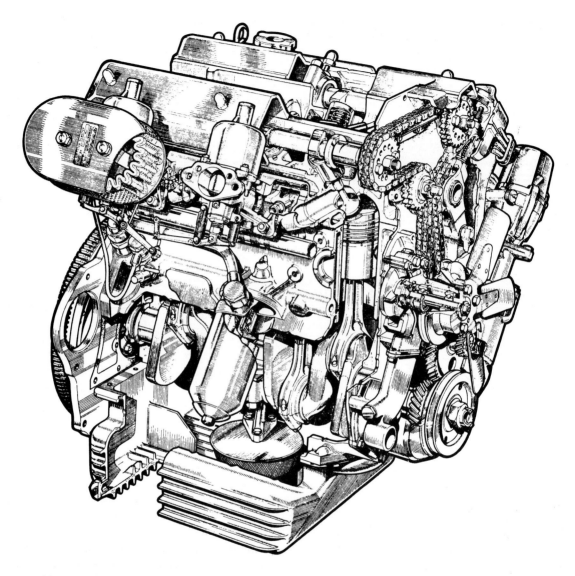

. . . and here in cutaway, showing the adaptation of the standard 'B' Series and the transfer of drive to the camshafts from gear at the crankshaft to chain at the camshafts.

chambers. The valves were angled at 80 degrees from each other, the inlets being 1.59in (40mm) in diameter, while the exhausts were 1.44in (37mm) across. The clean porting of this head ensured much better gas flow than the earlier 1,500cc pushrod engine and the hemispherical com-bustion chambers certainly made for a more efficient burn of the fuel/air mixture.

An SU electric fuel pump drew petrol from the rear-mounted 10 gallon (45 litre) tank and supplied it to a pair of Type H6 SU carburettors, each fitted with individual 'pancake' type air filters (which did little for the silencing of induction roar!). With a manual choke control for cold starting, these fed the mixture, through 0.010in size jets and Type OA6 needles, via a full four port inlet manifold to the combustion chambers. Sparks came from the crankcase front-mounted Lucas distributor to the 14mm plugs which, as in the pre-war Riley engine from which much of this cylinder head design came, were positioned just ahead of the transverse centre-line of the hemispherical combustion chambers. The resulting maximum power engine speed went up from 5,500 to 6,700rpm.

GEARED FOR PERFORMANCE

On its introduction, the MGA Twin-Cam was fitted with the same gearbox as that installed in the 1500 model. From the point of view of power and torque input, there was no reason why the original gearbox should not be used, as it was certainly up to the job, though the ratios of first, second and third gears were thought to be in need of review for use with this new engine of higher torque and much higher power. So, before long, a close ratio gear option was considered essential for the Twin-Cam.

The standard final drive ratio of 4.3:1 was also brought over from the original 1500 MGA to the Twin-Cam, so the top speed of the new model was derived almost entirely from an increase in engine speed, though a small contribution came from the slight increase in rolling circumference of the larger diameter tyres. That contribution was equal to seventeen road wheel revolutions per mile, so in a hypothetical one hour straight line run at 95mph (150km/h), the larger tyres would rotate 1,615 times less than the 5.60 × 15s of the 1,500cc version. This was, of course, another argument in the case for different gearing on the Twin-Cam.

Using the same ratios in the gearbox as for the pushrod MGA, the maximum road speeds in the gears were improved by 4mph (6km/h) in first gear, 8mph (12km/h) in second, 11mph (18km/h) in third and 17mph (27km/h) in top, the actual speeds in gears on test being 32, 53, 86 and 114mph (52, 85, 138 and 184km/h). This was the combined benefit of the Twin-Cam's higher engine speeds and the small benefit of the larger tyres, but it didn't remove the pleas from press and public alike for a closer ratio gearbox.

Quite early in the Twin-Cam's production life, the factory succumbed and a new set of closer ratios was made available in the MGA gearbox for the car, offered as an ex-works installed option in favour of the earlier close ratio gear clusters for self or specialist installation. This decision served two purposes for MG, the first being to provide the close ratios that many had been asking for and so (hopefully) improve sales and the second to remove the objection to gear cluster kits, where owners might not want (or be able) to fit their own close ratio sets – or afford the specialist to fit them. It was potentially quite an expensive exercise in any event for the private individual to install a close ratio set, so the catalogue option was particularly welcome.

Ratios in this new gearbox option were 5.449:1 for third gear (as opposed to 5.908 in the standard gearbox), 6.966:1 for second (versus 9.520 as standard) and 10.52:1 for first (against 15.652 with the original box). The corresponding road speed improvements in the intermediate gears were much improved, with 47mph (76km/h) in first, 72mph (116km/h) in second, 93mph (150km/h) in third and still 114mph (184km/h) in top. These compared very favourably with the speeds from the original gearbox, though the gap between first and second was still quite wide. With hindsight, it is a valid argument that a five-speed gearbox, had one been available, would have brought huge benefits.

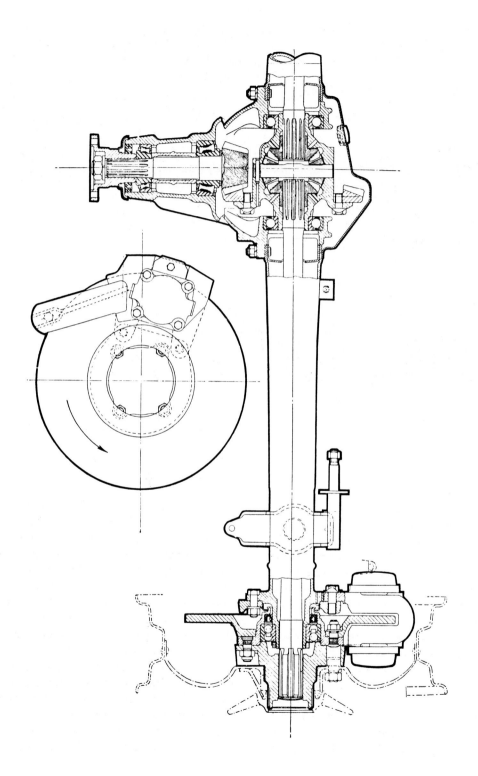

This drawing, from the MGA Twin-Cam service manual, shows the rear axle and handbrake arrangement for the Dunlop disc brakes. It also shows the centre-lock hub, with its peg drive instead of the more expensive (and in the long term less efficient) spline drive to the wheels.

Inside the Twin-Cam, the dashboard was vinyl covered; and at the same time as this new model was announced, so were the Deluxe seats, seen in this example, which made a significant improvement to comfort.

SETTING NEW STANDARDS

In many ways, the original MGA 1500 road-ster had already set a number of new standards for British sports cars. There are those who will say it took bits of its styling from the Jaguar XK120, though Alfa Romeo could have been just as influential. But while these may well have left an impression on Syd Enever and his design team, they are hardly likely to have been a major influence in the creation of the MGA. Indeed, the ultimate appearance of the EX182 cars showed a distinct originality which was the envy of many. It was less boxy than the Triumph TR2 and had much better interior draught exclusion than the Triumph, simply because of its door shape. Once the Twin-Cam engine was available in the MGA, its performance became quite comparable with that of the Triumph model, by now the TR3A, despite

the latter's 2.2-litre engine – but more of that in a later chapter.

Creature comfort was a distinct requirement in a sports car by 1958, certainly in the export markets in which MGAs were being sold. As a consequence of those comforts, cosmetic and real, being built in, the home market enjoyed the benefit too – when they could buy the cars, that is. One of the positive features of the MGA, when it was announced in 1955, was that it provided a much cosier ('user-friendly' in 1990s jargon) environment for both driver and passenger than many sports cars had done hitherto – even including the much more expensive Jaguar XK120 which, while well appointed inside, still used cutaway doors, providing the traditional 'elbow-room' for the driver.

The top door-line of the MGA drew much attention and comment from press and public alike when the car was first announced in

The scuttle vent badge, behind which now appears the 'Twin Cam' script . . .

. . . and the bootlid badge, also enhanced by the 'Twin Cam' wording.

1955. It set new standards in automotive design aerodynamics, though drag co-efficient had not yet become the sales feature that it was by the 1990s. But now, attention was turning to the inside of the car and, while the MGA scored quite highly here also, there were still odd things which could be done to improve the perception of driver and passenger comfort.

The first obvious cosmetic change to come with the MGA Twin-Cam was the vinyl covering to the dashboard, giving a softer impression and also taking away the cheap look of the earlier painted instrument panel, another point which had previously drawn criticism from road testers and buyers of the car. The heater, still an optional extra, was fitted to most Twin-Cams sold while carpets and trim were basically the same as in the 1500. The use of a padded roll around the cockpit of veteran aeroplanes was common, of course, as it was with certain vintage sports and racing cars. So it should come as no surprise that MG went one step further and covered the dash with vinyl, that principle leading to the full padded dashboards of modern sports cars.

The Dunlop disc wheel used on the MGA, which had already been proven at Le Mans on the 'D' Type Jaguars and on BRM Grand Prix cars.

The use of centre-lock steel disc wheels on the Twin-Cam was certainly a new standard in the world of volume-produced British sports cars and it was a change that was greeted with scepticism in certain quarters. However, the significantly greater strength of the Dunlop disc wheels had by now been well proven on several sports racing cars of the period and of course BMW had used centre-lock disc wheels both before and after the Second World War, while Jaguar had raced the 'D' Type and won at Le Mans on centre-lock steel wheels. For the MGA Twin-Cam's design team, there were the twin advantages of reduced unsprung weight and production costs held down.

It was already accepted that the MGA 1500 was a fine performer and a comfortable sports car. The Twin-Cam took those standards further, with its higher torque and power output, enabling a performance envelope closer to that designed for the chassis originally. This factor, combined with the improved comfort and interior trim brought this diminutive, perennially English sports car into competition for buyers' dollars with a most unusual market spectrum, competing at the lower end with the Alfa Romeo Giulietta Spyder, with its engine of 1,290cc, right up to the 4,324cc Chevrolet Corvette. Despite the wide variety, these cars competed because they were all in a similar price

Finally, the dashboard of the Twin-Cam. This one is nicely original, even down to the 'MG' key fob on the ignition key. The slot on the left of the dash is where the radio tuner was installed if the owner chose to have one fitted.

band and, while the Corvette clearly had far better maximum speed and acceleration figures to its credit, it didn't have the tautness of feel that the European cars had, so quite a number of would-be Corvette buyers actually ended up buying imports like the MGA Twin-Cam.

DEVELOPMENT OF THE TWIN-CAM

The original MGA Twin-Cam car was literally an adaptation of the pushrod-engined 1500, the first MGA. The Abingdon team simply took a 1957 1500 and replaced the engine with the new 1,588cc twin-overhead-cam unit. A pushrod version of the 1600, as it was to be called, had already been extensively bench- and road-tested and so the bottom half of the engine was proven and was intended to go into production for other cars in the BMC model range.

It's interesting to note that there were two sequences of valve timing in the engine's short production life. In the original timing sequence, the inlet valves opened at 35 degrees before top dead centre (BTDC) and closed at 65 degrees after bottom dead centre (ABDC), while the exhaust valves opened at 65 degrees before bottom dead centre (BBDC) and closed at 35 degrees after top dead centre (ATDC). This was soon changed and the timing quoted in the manufacturer's workshop manual gives inlet opening at 20 degrees BTDC, closing at 50 degrees ABDC, while exhaust opens at 50 degrees BBDC and closes at 20 degrees ATDC.

In addition to the standard timings offered by the manufacturer, there were, of course, options available from various engine specialists, but these were essentially offered as part of the preparation of a car for competitive use. Generally speaking, the state of tune of the production engine was perfectly adequate for road use, even for mild forms of

rallying and racing, activities in which the Twin-Cam figured extensively. It is, in fact, quite a compliment to the original design that many competing owners found the car met their needs without modification, though in the fuss of urban traffic, where most MGA Twin-Cams spent some part of their lives, regular attention was needed to prevent the engine from going off tune.

Of course, as modifications took place on the bodywork of the pushrod MGA, so they appeared on the Twin-Cam, as they shared a common body. Such little details as a relay for twin fog-lamps being fitted to cars for export to North America, then a modification to the door hinges, the windscreen hood pegs being made in mild steel instead of brass. Another metal change concerned the wheel nuts: firstly those on cars for Switzerland and Germany were changed for octagonal-shaped nuts instead of knock-ons and secondly, the knock-ons fitted to cars for other markets were made from bronze instead of mild steel. Then left-hand-drive cars destined for markets other than North America were fitted with a Centigrade marked temperature gauge instead of Fahrenheit. All these detail changes were incorporated into both Twin-Cam and pushrod models as they developed.

Stepping slightly ahead of this story for a moment, when the MGA 1600 replaced the original pushrod 1500 in May of 1959, so the revised body of that new variant was fitted to the Twin-Cam, updating it then to the same degree. Soon after that came a couple of export headlamp modifications, the first for the USA, where Lucas Mark VIII sealed beam units were fitted for cars to that market, while asymmetric headlamps appeared on cars for Sweden. Then a design change incorporated into the 1600 from the start of its production was embodied into the Twin-Cam. The road wheels were slightly modified to accommodate the front-wheel disc brakes, the differential was also changed and the half-shafts now had involute splines. With the advent of the Twin-Cam, the bonnet had been slightly bowed to clear the cam boxes and all subsequent MGAs were endowed with the revised bonnet. In addition to that, the 1600-bodied Twin-Cams also had removable inner wing panels as part of the process of standardizing body panels.

DEMISE OF THE TWIN-CAM

In retrospect, it is often said that the MGA Twin-Cam was only ever introduced to satisfy a limited, perhaps even specialist, market. The development path of the MGA suggests that this view is not entirely correct. It is certainly true that Abingdon could never really expect the Twin-Cam to outsell, or even equal, the sales level of the 1500 pushrod version, nor did it. However, it *was* reasonable to expect better sales than actually resulted.

That the Twin-Cam was not as reliable as it might have been is now a matter of record – they always needed regular tuning to keep the engine 'on song' and one modification introduced late in the car's life was aimed at helping solve that difficulty in some degree. This involved the modification in September 1959 of the air filter boxes to incorporate a venturi for improved breathing. In the opinion of some, the air space around the filters was so limited that it was thought to be a wonder the engine breathed as well as it did, for they were a very tight fit.

Of course, by late 1959 and early 1960 the Americans were becoming a little 'twitchy' about exhaust emissions and it was realized that the de-tuning of the Twin-Cam engine to clean up its exhaust to meet the likely emission standard requirements could well reduce the power output to that of a pushrod engine. The decision to standardize on the 1,600cc unit for all BMC models which used the 'B' Series engine was another factor and so, as the power output of the pushrod-engined MGA came closer to that of the Twin-Cam, the writing was on the wall.

Sales of the Twin-Cam had never been high volume, and while they were never intended to be so, it's reasonable to presume that the factory would have expected to make many more than the 2,000-odd total of roadsters and coupés actually built between 1958 and 1960. After all, production figures for the 1600 Coupé alone exceeded those for the Twin-Cam in all its forms. Only thirty-nine Twin-Cam Roadsters and twelve coupés were built in 1960, giving a clear sign that the pushrod 1600's price and the closeness of its performance were justification for would-be Twin-Cam buyers to forego the privilege of owning that model in favour of the new 1600. Maintenance was also a factor in the export markets at which the Twin-Cam was aimed, since a pushrod engine demanded far less attention and so cost less to keep on the road. The Twin-Cam, despite being a thoroughly exciting car when 'on song', was not endowed with a particularly strong reliability record. One key reason for the 8.3:1 compression ratio change was that high-compression pistons had holed on several occasions in service, presenting rather high warranty repair bills to the dealer network. As a consequence, the last Twin-Cam (Chassis Number 2611) left the Abingdon factory in June 1960.

6 How the Twin-Cam was Received

The MGA Twin-Cam introduced a new standard to the world of small sports cars in Great Britain, in that it was the first overhead-cam-engined sports car in its price bracket since the end of the Second World War. It was also the first MG car to have a twin-cam engine of any kind, but more importantly, it set the pace for the whole future of moderately priced sports cars made in Britain – and, for that matter, much of Europe.

In post-war years, there hadn't been a reasonably priced twin-cam two-seat sports car before the MGA Twin-Cam, so it should not be surprising that in some circles it was likened, by those with the experience to remember, to the pre-war British Salmson, Squire or the Riley Sprite. All three cars had been powered by 1500cc twin-cam engines, the Squire and Salmson being twin overhead camshafts, the Riley's mounted high in the cylinder block, using short pushrods as the

From the collection of the late Bob Gerard comes this picture of himself and his wife Joan in what many regarded as the the car which the MGA Twin-Cam succeeded – the Riley Sprite.

This beautiful MGA Twin-Cam (with standard seats, it will be noted) was everything in 1958 that the Riley was in 1938. This magnificent example belongs to Larry Wilson, of Alliance, Ohio.

medium of valve actuation. The Squire was, of course, a very expensive machine, the Salmson and Riley less so. But the market slot occupied by these cars had not been filled since the end of the war. Now the twin-cam-engined MGA was to fill it admirably.

In mainland Europe, of course, there were several small sports cars offered in direct competition to the MGA, but the one car which stood out as the real adversary was a car which forfeited 200cc of engine capacity, though little else except price. This was the Alfa Romeo Giulietta Spyder, a magnificent little car which, in post-war years, was the nearest thing anyone ever came to producing what was a true substitute for the pre-war Riley Nine sporting saloons and two-seaters.

The Giulietta had first been sprung on a surprised market in 1954, the Sprint Coupe and Berlina (saloon) being the first versions out of the factory gates. By 1955, the same year as the 1,500cc pushrod-engined MGA was announced, Alfa Romeo and Pininfarina had completed their work and were ready to release the Spyder. This 80bhp, 1,290cc twin-cam-engined little marvel was capable of just over 100mph (165km/h) in original form, whilst the Spyder Veloce, produced a year later, went up to a cool 112mph (180km/h) still on 1,290cc, but now producing 90bhp at 6,500rpm, a rather higher engine speed than even the Twin-Cam MGA.

The car everybody said the MGA, especially the Twin-Cam, had to beat – the Alfa Romeo Giulietta Spyder. Well, the Alfa was still a bit quicker even than the Twin-Cam, but the MG was a lot less money.

FIRST VIEWS OF THE TWIN-CAM

The 'New Cars Described' feature of *The Autocar* magazine in Britain contained the first detailed account of the Twin-Cam, and the author of the article gave a pretty accurate account of what was to come, with excellent cross-section and cutaway drawings, as well as photographs to illustrate the merits of the new engine. From the underside, the cylinder head looked remarkably like that of the already mentioned Riley Sprite engine, but that should hardly be surprising in view of the man who led the design team responsible for it.

The Autocar spoke highly of the design characteristics of the Twin-Cam engine, noting the heavier-section connecting rods, the higher-capacity oil pump and, oddly enough, the fact that the crankcase was cast from entirely new patterns, despite the fact that it had to comply dimensionally with the specification of the standard 'B' Series BMC unit. The article made quite a point of the fact, however, that machining of the MGA Twin-Cam block could take place on the line at Longbridge, so greatly reducing the machining costs, which would otherwise have been prohibitive. Bearing sizes were the same, too, again saving a large element of cost.

The article went on to comment on the new Dunlop disc brakes and centre-lock disc wheels from the same manufacturer, praising both, one for the inevitable improvement in stopping power, the other for the reduction in weight it gave to the car, while endowing it with wheels which were much stronger than wires, yet still of centre-lock type, thus quick removal and installation were available at much lower unsprung weight. Power comparisons showed the Twin-Cam to be streets ahead of its pushrod ancestor in both brake horsepower and torque output, so the first verdict was that the new car was a very sound investment for £843, plus an abundance of taxes which increased the ultimate selling price by over 50 per cent!

EARLY ROAD TESTS

The Autocar also published one of the first road tests of the Twin-Cam, which was carried in the same issue as the 'New Cars Described' feature of 18 July 1958. No doubt this road test was conducted in the wake of the press test day organized by BMC at the War Department's Fighting Vehicles Research and Development Establishment at Chobham, where *Sports Cars Illustrated*'s reviewer concluded that it was potentially a tremendous sports car, and lamented that it was not to be available to the home market for quite a long time after its announcement, due to Britain's need for the cash benefits of exports.

The road test vehicle which *The Autocar* put through its paces was a right-hand-drive model (PMO326) and was probably the car that John Ferguson had laboured over for hours in the production of his superb drawings of the car's various characteristics, though it was not the car *Sports Cars Illustrated* drove at Chobham, for that was PMO946 – a relevant observation from the point of view of the unanimity of the conclusions drawn. Both road testers were lavish in their praise of the new model's braking performance and handling. Both spoke well of the engine's responsiveness and power, the slick gear-change allowing the impressive torque to be used to best advantage.

One thing that *The Autocar* did latch on to was the limited accessibility of the under-bonnet space, commenting that many ancillaries were hard to get at, such as the distributor and the coil, the former being lodged underneath a camshaft housing, while the latter was hidden under the heater trunking. The oil dipstick was criticized for its length – a little longer would have made it easily accessible – as it was, it was awkward to reach and relocate. The reviewer was also unhappy about the lack of an oil temperature gauge. The fact that no car in this price bracket had been fitted with one up to now was not a consideration; the test car had an oil cooler, so it should have a temperature gauge to go with it.

American reviewers seemed to think that the styling of the MGA had an Italian flavour to it, though it was positively all-Abingdon. That said, while it was not an intentional or conscious act to give a particular likeness to anything else, the car certainly had a few features quite similar to the Austin Healey 100. For example, the profile of both cars showed a low, sweeping line running from the arch of the front wing down to the rear of the door (the top of which formed part of that line), then rising gently over the rear wheels. At the front, both cars also had their radiator

CONDITIONS
Weather: Warm and dry, light wind. (Temperature 52°–61°F., Barometer 30.0–30.1 in. Hg.) Surface: Dry concrete Autobahn (acceleration and maximum speed tests). Dry concrete banked track for fuel consumption tests.
Fuel: German pump fuel, approx. 97 Research Method Octane Number (acceleration and maximum speed tests), 100 R.M.O.N. elsewhere.

INSTRUMENTS
Speedometer at 30 mph	2% fast
Speedometer at 60 mph	6% slow
Speedometer at 90 mph	4% slow
Distance recorder	3% slow

WEIGHT
Kerb weight (unladen, but with oil, coolant and fuel for approx. 50 miles)	19cwt
Front/rear distribution of kerb weight	53½/46½
Weight laden as tested	23 cwt

MAXIMUM SPEEDS
Flying Quarter Mile
Mean of four opposite runs	113.0 mph
Best one-way time equals	115.0 mph

'Maximile' speed. (Timed quarter mile after one mile accelerating from rest.)
Mean of four opposite runs	101.3 mph
Best one-way time equals	104.2 mph

Speed in Gears. (at 6,500 rpm recommended limit).
Max. speed in 3rd gear	81 mph
Max. speed in 2nd gear	50 mph
Max. speed in 1st gear	31 mph

FUEL CONSUMPTION
Top gear
37 mpg at constant 30 mph on level
36½ mpg at constant 40 mph on level
33½ mpg at constant 50 mph on level
32½ mpg at constant 60 mph on level
29½ mpg at constant 70 mph on level
22 mpg at constant 90 mph on level
17½ mpg at constant 100 mph on level

Overall Fuel Consumption for 1,593 miles, 71.7 gallons equals 22.2 mpg (12.7 litres/100 km)

Touring Fuel Consumption (mpg at steady speed midway between 30 mph and maximum, less 5% allowance for acceleration) 27.6

Fuel tank capacity (maker's figure) 10 gallons.

STEERING
Turning circle between kerbs:	
Left	31 feet
Right	30 feet
Turns of steering wheel from lock to lock	2¾

ACCELERATION TIMES from standstill
0–30 mph	2.6 sec
0–40 mph	4.4 sec
0–50 mph	7.3 sec
0–60 mph	9.1 sec
0–70 mph	12.3 sec
0–80 mph	16.2 sec
0–90 mph	24.6 sec
0–100 mph	40.3 sec
Standing quarter mile	18.1 sec

Acceleration times on upper ratios
	Top gear	3rd gear
10–30 mph	—	8.3 sec
20–40 mph	10.7 sec	6.5 sec
30–50 mph	9.7 sec	6.5 sec
40–60 mph	8.8 sec	5.5 sec
50–70 mph	9.4 sec	5.5 sec
60–80 mph	13.9 sec	8.3 sec
70–90 mph	15.2 sec	—
80–100 mph	23.1 sec	—
90–110 mph	—	—

HILL CLIMBING at sustained steady speeds
Max gradient on top gear
     1 in 9.3 (Tapley 240lb/ton)
Max gradient on 3rd gear
     1 in 6.6 (Tapley 335lb/ton)
Max gradient on 2nd gear
     1 in 4.0 (Tapley 545lb/ton)

BRAKES
0.90g retardation (equivalent to 33½ ft. stopping distance) with 100 lb. pedal pressure.
0.80g retardation (equivalent to 37½ ft. stopping distance) with 80 lb. pedal pressure.
0.51g retardation (equivalent to 59 ft. stopping distance) with 50 lb. pedal pressure.
0.32g retardation (equivalent to 94 ft. stopping distance) with 25 lb. pedal pressure.

One of the earliest comprehensive road tests on the Twin-Cam was performed by The Motor, *whose test table is reproduced here.*

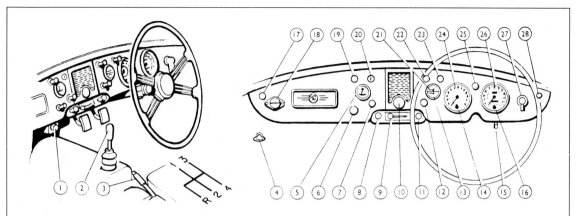

1, Headlamp dip switch. 2, Gear lever. 3, Handbrake. 4, Bonnet catch release. 5, Fuel contents gauge.
6, Windscreen washer button. 7, Choke control. 8, Ventilator control. 9, Heater control and fan switch. 10, Horn
button. 11, Demister control. 12, Starter switch. 13, Water thermometer. 14, Dynamo charge warning light. 15,
Trip resetting knob. 16, Headlamp main beam indicator. 17, Map reading light switch. 18, Map reading light.
19, Windscreen wipers switch. 20, Ignition switch. 21, Oil pressure gauge. 22, Lights switch. 23, Foglamp switch.
24, Rev. counter. 25, Panel light switch. 26, Speedometer and distance recorder. 27, Direction indicator switch.
28, Direction indicator warning light.

grilles identifying the car, but set into the front panel and forming part of the aero-dynamic shape, while the sweep down of the rear wing and boot lid followed the same line to give a clean air-penetrating shape long before the term 'drag co-efficient' became fashionable.

The Austin Healey 100 Series and the MGA were individual cars, each clearly identifiable from the other, yet showing a similarity of line which suggested the same basic school of styling thought – a distinctly English school of thought at that.

ON THE ROAD WITH THE PRESS

Back to *The Autocar*; their road tester was clearly not the sort of person taken in by the pretty line of a new car, or by the claim of performance without proof. With this car, the performance claim certainly *was* backed up now, so the conversion kit merchants would have little to do for the Twin-Cam

MGA. Even so, our reviewer found a loose baffle in the silencer and was disturbed by the background mechanical noise, largely tappets enhanced by the thrash of timing gears and chains.

The Autocar tester found the engine lumpy, lacking the smoothness of the six-cylinder engine which had now found its way into the Austin Healey 100 for example, but it wasn't short on power. With 9.9:1 compression ratio and only four cylinders, it was hardly likely to be a silken runner, but on the other hand, the exhaust noise was not found to be offensive, even bouncing off the buildings of city streets, and induction roar was found to be minimal, despite the small pancake-type air cleaners.

The easy-starting engine was also free-revving and while a little lumpy at low speeds, once it had reached 3,000rpm, it quickly picked up and would run to maximum power with ease. The original gearing allowed it to pull the car up to a very respectable cruise speed of 80–90mph (130–145km/h) in an equally respectable

In profile, the MGA was thought by some to have quite 'Italian' styling and many preferred its lines to those of the Alfa, regardless of price.

time. *The Autocar*'s road tester also ran the car for 5 miles (8km) at maximum speed (on a Belgian *Autoroute* – there were too few British highways available then to allow anything near 100mph (160km/h) for as much as 5 miles (8km) distance), showing 6,500rpm on the rev counter, without any sign of strain, but he did notice a vibration at 5,500rpm. Even so, it seems the engine took 7,000rpm regularly with ease.

Because this early road test car still used the same gearing as the original pushrod 1500 MGA, *The Autocar*'s correspondent was drawn to the expected conclusion (one which had been drawn when the 1500 was road tested some two years before) that there was too wide a gap between its first and second gears, as well as between second and third. Close ratio gear clusters had been available as conversions, but this road test was another clear indication that a standard close ratio option needed to be offered as a factory listed item.

Odd nit-picking apart, the reviewer was clearly impressed by the handling of the Twin-Cam, remarking that the road-holding and cornering of this new MGA were among its most delightful features. It should be remembered that the car's running gear was virtually unchanged, the steering rack having been moved slightly forward and minor linkage changes being made. The turning circle was greater on the Twin-Cam than the 1500, being now 32ft 6in (9.9m), whereas the original car had a turning circle of only 28ft (8.5m). With two-and-three-quarter turns from lock to lock, it didn't seem to make too much difference to the high- or low-speed handling of the car, parking in confined spaces being said to be no problem.

Out on the open road, where the Twin-Cam was really able to be put through its paces, engine power, albeit conveyed by less-than-ideal gearing, combined with superb cornering (*The Autocar*'s reviewer found remarkably little roll and wholly predictable

Under the bonnet, the Twin-Cam engine was a tight fit and nothing was easily accessible, except perhaps the oil filler!

tail-slide) and braking to match anything on the road at the time. We have come to expect high standards of brakes on everyday cars built today, but disc brakes were only just coming into use on cars in this value bracket in the 1950s. As a consequence, the MGA Twin-Cam was listed as a high performer in the braking department, thus justifying the Abingdon by-line 'Safety Fast' in full.

Under test, the braking performance of the Twin-Cam drew no criticisms whatsoever. Even at 100mph (160km/h), the car's Dunlop discs were judged to be capable of doing all that was asked of them in dry or wet weather. The pedal pressure essential to bringing the car down from high speeds was said to be a little high, as there was no self-servo effect, though it wasn't thought to be

The Twin-Cam was soon popular on the track, too, and here P.J. McCallum charges away from the opposition in a club event at Brands Hatch.

especially hard underfoot, nor did it become spongy with use. Slamming the pedal down from maximum speed to stop brought the car to a standstill four-square, with no hint of deviation from a straight line. Even after 800 miles (1,300km) of hard and fast driving, there was no perceptible brake fade or increase in pedal travel. One thing that was noticeable, however, was the actual pedal pressure needed to bring the car to as abrupt a halt as it was capable of from 30mph (50km/h). To achieve the best stopping distance of 32½ feet (9.9m), some 90lb (40kg) of pedal pressure was necessary.

The conclusion of this road test was that the MGA Twin-Cam was a worthy development of the basic MGA model, a car which maximized the performance potential of the chassis, enhanced by the addition of disc brakes, but still possessed of some of the shortcomings manifested in the original version. Particularly, the need for improved interior ventilation around the feet was noted, as was the limited vision at night

when the car was being driven at high speeds. Also, a hand-operated dip-switch was thought to be preferable to the existing foot-type, as would have been two-speed wipers for the windscreen. But, on balance, this was thought to be a car which held up well the name and reputation of MG.

FIRST IMPRESSIONS IN NORTH AMERICA

The American magazine *Sports Cars Illustrated* (*SCI*) managed to get hold of a Twin-Cam MGA in the late summer of 1958 and subjected it to a pretty exhaustive road test. It was one of the first cars off the boat and was probably set up to run richer than it might have been in optimum tune, so as to minimize the risk of early damage, bearing in mind that the distance between the factory and the car could have been up to 7,000 miles (11,000km)! *SCI* was one of those more thorough magazines than might be perceived

---

John W. Thornley OBE (1909-1994)

John Thornley was Director & General Manager of MG when the MGA was created and put into production. His first connection with MG was in 1930, when he became the first secretary of the newly formed MG Car Club. He was then an accountancy student and within a year was employed at Abingdon. Appointed Service Manager of the MG Car Company in 1934, Thornley managed the 'Three Musketeers' and 'Cream Cracker' trials teams, creating an acceptability for himself that might not have been accorded many another accountant, for they were car people at Abingdon, not administrators or 'bean counters'.

After reaching the rank of Lieutenant-Colonel in the Royal Army Ordnance Corps during the Second World War, John Thornley was re-appointed Service Manager upon his return, then from Sales and Service Manager to Assistant General Manager. After the transfer of Riley from Coventry to Abingdon in 1948/9, a Riley man was made MG General Manager, an appointment greeted with some suspicion by many, though it was short lived as Jack Tatlow made his mark as a straight-speaking operator who was first and foremost a motor man. In many ways, it was Jack Tatlow who laid the ground for the appointment of his successor, John Thornley, who took up the post in 1952.

MG and Riley production peaked at just under 13,700 cars in 1952 as John Thornley became General Manager and the factory's prosperity improved as Britain's motor industry grew in the 1950s. MGs were raced and rallied with factory support and their engines were used by such small sports car specialists as Lotus and Cooper. This was also the year in which Nuffield and Austin merged to create, for a while, the third largest motor manufacturing enterprise in the world. It was that year also in which Syd Enever's new sports car design, EX175, was first presented to the new group board at Longbridge, with John Thornley's enthusiastic support.

It is said that Thornley's tenacity and enthusiasm were the principal factors in winning the battle for approval of the MGA's production. That same tenacity and enthusiasm was responsible for the approval of the Twin-Cam, using the design created by Eddie Maher's team as the basis for the most cost-effective option of the two variations offered, winning for them a proving opportunity in the 1955 Tourist Trophy Race. There's no doubt that John Thornley's presence was a major benefit in the process of bringing the MGA from racing special to production sports car.

John Thornley died in July 1994 after a long battle with heart disease.

---

as average, because they loved to take cars to bits and modify them. In this case, no modifications were carried out in the October 1958 road test, though they concluded the Twin-Cam gave a performance roughly equal to that of a Stage 4-tuned pushrod 1500 MGA.

By the time their December 1958 issue was out, *SCI* had gone to work on the suspension and running gear of the Twin-Cam, to improve what they called the 'raceability' of the car (*SCI*'s prime interest being in the competition sector, at which it aimed its publication). They stiffened up the front suspension, reduced the weight by around 80lb (35kg) (how is not revealed, but they probably slung out the hood, sidescreens and spare wheel cover to begin with), then fitted Dunlop R3 racing tyres (illegal on the road even then, but they clearly didn't worry about that!) and a works optional close ratio gearbox. This reduced their lap time at Lime Rock Park racing circuit by 1½ seconds, but *SCI* was looking for something significantly better than that.

June 1959 saw *SCI* back in print about the Twin-Cam. This time they had sought, and been given, permission from importers Hambro Automotive, to strip down the engine and 'breathe' on it, but only on condition that they did not modify it beyond production specification and that they did not quote any of the resulting performance figures as official or officially approved. So, the car was trotted down to *SCI*'s favourite local workshop and the engine was stripped down, everything being measured on the way. This really was road-testing 'from the inside out'.

What was discovered in the strip-down was reported back to Hambro and then published for consumption by *SCI*'s readership. It must be said that the engine was reported to be one produced on the line at BMC's Longbridge Engines Plant, as part of a pre-production batch put on the line at Longbridge to test the viability of manufacturing a twin-cam engine in a mass production facility alongside the 'B' Series pushrod units. Well, it proved possible, but our American friends discovered a few things that proved ultimately helpful in longer term manufacture. Firstly, the camshafts were the early type (35/65/65/35 degree timing) and so were replaced with the later ones of 20/50/50/20 degree timing.

When the pistons were removed, they gave our correspondents quite a surprise, as they were badly scuffed. This was put down to the fact that they were solid-skirt pistons with a very close clearance of 0.035in. *SCI* concluded that this, combined with the use of SAE40-grade Castrol 'R' oil to run in the engine, was wholly responsible for the extent of engine wear they found, for the bores had also been worn out by four thousandths of an inch by the hard chrome top rings on the pistons. It said something for the quality of the pistons that they were all still intact.

In the process of re-assembly of the engine, *SCI* obtained new pistons from Hambro Automotive. These which were different from those removed in that the rings were positioned closer together and there were no oil vent holes below the ring slots (these were now just behind the oil control ring, within

the slot for the ring itself). An iron ring replaced the hard chrome top one on each piston and when the engine was re-bored, as it had to be, the cold clearance between piston wall and cylinder bore was doubled from thirty-five to seventy thousands of an inch. Everything was then balanced and put back together. All sharp edges on the cylinder head (even those around the spark plug holes) were removed and then ports and combustion chambers were polished. Next the new camshafts were fitted and valve clearances increased slightly from the 0.018in quoted.

With the engine back in the car, off went our intrepid road testers. Hardly surprisingly, they found the torque output below 3,000rpm pretty poor, but once over 3,500rpm, the car fairly rocketed at the touch of the throttle. They related one occasion when, on a straight piece of road, there was a car about half a mile ahead, with a bend in the road about a quarter of a mile further on. Concluding that the car in front would be round the bend before they reached him, they stabbed the throttle, only to find themselves clawing for braking effort as they were about to crawl all over him long before they reached the bend. *SCI* was clearly impressed!

OTHER VIEWS FROM THE GREAT CONTINENT

A magazine called *Speed Age*, published in the United States, gave a page to the Twin-Cam in its November 1958 issue. It's opening line read:

Heartily tired of their product looking down the twin tailpipes of Porsches on the world's road circuits, the men of Abingdon-on-Thames have turned their popular, but innocuous, MGA into what bids fair to become a raging Porsche killer.

Whether or not the Twin-Cam became a 'raging Porsche killer' is discussed in another chapter of this book, but the point was well made that this new MGA was certainly notably better in performance and power than its predecessor, the 1,500cc pushrod-engined MGA. *Speed Age* went on to describe all the now-familiar features which distinguished the Twin-Cam from its forebear – the twin-cam engine of course, the disc brakes, the centre-lock disc wheels, the leatherette-covered dashboard. It said nothing of the odd shortcomings mentioned by other publications, most probably because *Speed Age* didn't actually get to do a full road test. That didn't really matter, though, because the magazine had only praise for the new model and so added to the growing appeal of this fine little British sports car in North America.

The mighty *Road and Track* was next to offer a view of the Twin-Cam. *Road and Track* was already fast becoming the most respected sports car magazine in the United States, something of an American version of Britain's *Motor Sport*. It was California-based and staffed by a group of very pro-European sports car journalists. In fact, they probably did more for Britain's export drive than many car distributors, extolling the virtues and handling characteristics of many a 'Brit-mobile' over homebuilt machinery.

R & T, as it is known internationally, got its hands on a Twin-Cam in time for its November 1958 issue, along with a number of its competitors, though they didn't go to the lengths *Sports Cars Illustrated* went to and did not extend their test to a total strip-down. *R & T* has always had a reputation for being precise and cautious about its road test reviews, to the extent that it challenged the findings of a British magazine, suggesting that the car they had tested was probably not truly representative of what the buyer could expect from his production car.

After the usual descriptive preamble out-lining the specification of the Twin-Cam and stating its particular virtues, *R & T* got down to business and compared two cars, one with the standard gearbox and 4.3:1 rear axle ratio, the other with the optional lower final drive ratio of 4.55:1 and the factory optional close-ratio gearbox. They charted the performance figures of the standard version and matched them to those produced by both *Motor* and *The Autocar* in Britain. One interesting comparison was the time it took for the car to reach 80mph (129km/h) on the *R & T* test and the speeds logged by the other two. *R & T* took 18.1 seconds to reach 80 from a standing start and was still in third gear. One of the other two logged 72mph (116km/h), in third, while the other made it to 83mph (134km/h), just changing into fourth in the same time.

Once again, braking was found to be impeccable in both versions tested, with virtually no fade or increase in pedal travel after a hard drive. And it was a hard drive, for they managed to wring a 10-second-flat 0–60mph time, where virtually everyone else in North America was over that time, though *Motor* at home had recorded a 9.1-second run. There was no doubt, however, that the lower geared version of the Twin-Cam performed better for *R&T* and so that was the version they recommended to their readers – which is probably why the vast majority of US-specification Twin-Cams are, in fact, equipped with the 4.55:1 rear axle.

R & T's final observations were varied. They liked the slightly heavier clutch pedal action, as much as anything else because the clutch didn't slip throughout the test. They liked the rev limit, though rarely went above 6,500rpm. They liked the power and torque, because it now justified everything else about the MGA. They liked the brakes and wheels, but not the increased weight of the car. They were apprehensive about the lack of servo assistance on the brake pedal, but didn't find it an undue problem.

MG A TWIN CAM

SPECIFICATIONS

List price	$3345
Curb weight	2200
Test weight	2480
distribution, %	53/47
Dimensions, length	156
width	58
height	50
Wheelbase	94.0
Tread, f and r	47.9/48.9
Tire size	5.90–15
Brake lining area	32
Steering, turns	2.7
turning circle	32
Engine type	4 cly, dohc
Bore & stroke	2.97 x 3.50
Displacement, cu in	96.9
cc	1588
Compression ratio	9.90
BHP @ rpm	108 @ 6700
equivalent mph	118.1
Torque, lb-ft	104 @ 4500
equivalent mph	79.4

GEAR RATIOS

O/d (n.a.), overall	
4th (1.000)	4.30
3rd (1.374)	5.91
2nd (2.214)	9.52
1st (3.640)	15.7

CALCULATED DATA

Lb/hp (test wt)	23.0
Cu ft/ton mile	76.8
Mph/1000 rpm (4th)	17.6
engine revs/mile	3400
Piston travel, ft/mile	1985
Rpm @ 2500 ft/min	4280
equivalent mph	75.5
R&T wear index	67.5

PERFORMANCE

Top speed (6400), mph	113
best timed run	115
3rd (7000)	90
2nd (7000)	56
1st (7000)	34

FUEL CONSUMPTION

Normal range, mpg	15/24

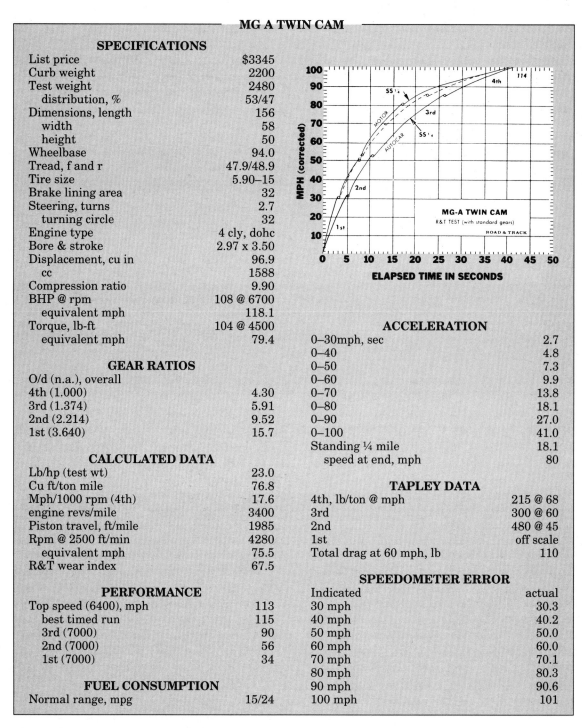

ACCELERATION

0–30mph, sec	2.7
0–40	4.8
0–50	7.3
0–60	9.9
0–70	13.8
0–80	18.1
0–90	27.0
0–100	41.0
Standing ¼ mile	18.1
speed at end, mph	80

TAPLEY DATA

4th, lb/ton @ mph	215 @ 68
3rd	300 @ 60
2nd	480 @ 45
1st	off scale
Total drag at 60 mph, lb	110

SPEEDOMETER ERROR

Indicated	actual
30 mph	30.3
40 mph	40.2
50 mph	50.0
60 mph	60.0
70 mph	70.1
80 mph	80.3
90 mph	90.6
100 mph	101

Road & Track *also thought well of the Twin-Cam. It is interesting to compare their road test data table with that of* The Motor.

The MGA 1500 was the first of the line and that it was so little changed as new variants were developed is testament to the success of its design, in an age when annual models were still common. (Inset:) The radiator grille.

Some of the most attractive front end designs of cars are let down by the treatment of the rear end, but not so with the MGA.

The Twin-Cam Roadster was the first development of the MGA after the introduction of the basic 1500. This elegant example shows how good the MGA can look in black.

This shot of a Twin-Cam's front disc brake and road wheel shows clearly the drive pegs on the inner face of the wheel and the slots in the hub.

Deluxe seats and the vinyl-covered dash in the Twin-Cam make the interior an altogether more comfortable environment for the car's occupants.

There are only two tell-tale features which identify the Twin-Cam from the 1500, the badge on the bootlid which tells you it's a Twin-Cam and the centre-lock disc wheels. This is the end of the Twin-Cam most other motorists saw on the road.

The Twin-Cam Coupé was the rarest of all MGAs and is, of course, the most desirable version today. This is a later series Twin-Cam, with the same body style as the 1600, as evidenced by the tail-lights.

In profile, the 1600 Roadster shows the body it shares with the later Twin-Cam, though this one enjoys wire wheels instead of the standard four-stud discs.

The wire wheel option available on the 1600, a roadster in this case.

Behind the seats lies the bag containing the sidescreens. This is a 1600, with the sliding-window type sidescreens.

Also behind the seat is the ring-pull lever which opens the boot, a characteristic much-criticised by road testers and reviewers, as it offered no real security for the contents of the boot and was inconvenient to use.

The 1600 Mark II was, of course, the final form of the MGA and this very attractive example, a wire-wheeled coupé, shows the sheer grace of line of the MGA Coupé – a true classic.

Head on, the Mark II doesn't look a lot different from the first MGA 1600, unless you look closely for the revised grille.

Under the bonnet, a superbly clean 1600 engine also looks little different from the 1500, except for the air cleaners and the positioning of certain ancillary items.

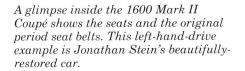

The tail of the Mark II lets you know its identity by the '1600 Mk II' badging and the horizontal tail-light cluster, with its amber direction indicators. The tail lights are probably the least attractive feature of the Mark II.

A glimpse inside the 1600 Mark II Coupé shows the seats and the original period seat belts. This left-hand-drive example is Jonathan Stein's beautifully-restored car.

A follower's view of Jonathan Stein's car shows the practicality of the late-type tail-lights, with amber flashing direction indicators on the outer end of the horizontal arrangement. The Pennsylvania countryside could just as easily be south Oxfordshire.

The brochure which launched the MGA Twin-Cam in the summer of 1958.

All in all, *Road and Track* thought the MGA Twin-Cam a tremendous step forward for Abingdon and recommended the car very highly. They credited the development of the Twin-Cam to a desire to do better on the race tracks and in North America, which was probably not far off the mark. They thought the car would do well – history tells us that it did, by and large – but also that the Twin-Cam would not displace the pushrod-engined car from its market position. This was a view no doubt borne in mind when it came to Abingdon's deliberations about the next stage in the MGA's longer term development.

MOTOR SHOWS AND REFLECTIONS

The motor show circuit for the MGA Twin-Cam began with Earls Court in London, where thousands of sports-car starved enthusiasts clamoured to get a view of this new version of a car they'd almost not believed a couple of years before. The novelty

97

of the MGA shape had more or less worn off by now, but the new engine brought all the plaudits back and created in the public eye an image of a truly up-to-date sports car – a car for the second half of the twentieth century, in mechanical specification as well as in style. While the power now matched that of the pushrod 2-litre Triumph TR3, the dashing line of the MGA, with its BRM-style disc wheels, and the charisma of a twin-cam engine, was far more of an attraction to many would-be buyers.

In motor show after motor show, the MGA Twin-Cam was acclaimed as the new British challenge to such cars as the Porsche 356 and the Alfa Romeo Giulietta Spyder. It was also to be compared with the Lotus Elite, which was not a true comparison, partly because the Elite was a 1,100cc car, partly because it was a kit car (in Britain, though not in export markets) and, of course, it was a coupé, not an open two-seater. But then, there was by now a coupé version of the MGA. . .

7 Coupé or Roadster?

When anyone says MG, you immediately think of open sports cars, don't you? After all, isn't the very epitome of the MG a spartan, open car in which comfort is sacrificed to performance? It may then come as a surprise to some, perhaps, to learn that MG coupés were built in the early 1930s, in the days when MG was a rising star after its tremendous performance in the 1930 Junior Car Club 'Double Twelve' at Brooklands.

Most pre-war MG coupés were built by specialist coachbuilders on MG chassis, though Abingdon had catalogued coupés among its range since the early 1930s, including the M-Type Midget, the Magna, the P-Type Airline and the rare, but well

publicized T-Type Airline Coupé. Sportsmen's coupés had secured a following since the earliest post-First World War days when cars had become more accessible to the potential owner-driver. After all, not everybody wanted to get cold or wet as part of the privilege of driving and enjoying a sports car.

THE CREATION OF A COUPÉ

All too often, when a car maker decides to make a coupé version of a production roadster, the compromises in shape which result from the 'tacking-on' of a top manage to spoil the line of what was otherwise an attractive

For some time before the factory decided to produce a coupé version the MGA, various component manufacturers were offering detachable hardtops, of which this is one example. It was always important to show how easy it was to fit and remove, so two young ladies in summer frocks were used to demonstrate the point that you could do the job easily and cleanly!

The prototype Coupé was ULJ426, seen here on display. There were several feature differences between this and the production Coupé, including the door pillar, the glazing of the rear window and the thickness of the bottom sill of the coupé top at the rear.

sports car. Frequently, the coupé top looks like a separate hard-top stuck on, and misses its point in the process. The MGA Coupé was one of those rare examples of careful design which worked first time. It looked almost as though the original MGA had been designed as a coupé from the start, so well integrated was the new top.

Announced in 1956, the MGA 1500 Coupé went into series production the following year, by the end of which there were more than 4,000 on the roads of the world, over 3,250 of them going to North America. The careful re-jigging of the scuttle pressing to accommodate the windscreen pillars, the deeper wrap-round windscreen, the skilfully blended-in roof line and revamped doors all combined to make a superb purpose-built coupé. Locking doors, wind-up windows and a wide rear window made it a weather-tight cosy vehicle with superb all-round vision.

MAKING THE DREAM COME TRUE

Construction of the MGA Coupé was relatively simple. It was, essentially, a hard-top, but permanently attached rather than clipped on as a proprietary hard-top would have been.

The roof was a single pressing, which may not seem particularly special at first glance, until you look at the depth of the pressing and the curvature in the front pillars and rear quarter panels. It says as much for the skill of the press tool designer, who managed to produce a crease-free pressing, as for its designer, Eric Carter, who managed to produce a coupé top that looked as though it was an integral part of the original MGA design. The roof panel was welded into place around the rear bottom rail, from the front of each rear quarter panel and via the windscreen pillars at the front. A sealing strip, which was painted the same colour as the car, ran around the weld line of the roof (which was also leaded), where it joined the panel of the rear deck.

Inside the mounted roof pressing was a reinforcing assembly of sub-pressings, including a pair of quite substantial inner screen pillars. Apart from giving additional strength to the roof, they also served as mountings for the interior trim and the upper door seals. The windscreen had a much deeper curve to it than that of the roadster and the rear screen wrapped round to give a superb rear view for the driver, though if the car looked the slightest bit ungainly from any quarter, this was it. It wasn't helped by the fact that the rear screen was a three-piece unit set into a one-piece rubber

surround which required more than a little skill to install. If those two vertical rubber pillars, thin as they were, had not been there to break the horizontal line, it may well have looked a little cleaner and a little less ungainly.

The quite deep door pockets which were a feature of the original MGA door design (and quite appreciated by many owners for storage of all sorts of things in addition to maps) were now to disappear, to make way for the window mechanism to raise and lower the side windows which replaced the sidescreens that went with the hood of the roadster. The door pressing itself was a modification of the original, adding a short riser from the top line as a mounting for the wind-up window guide and rain seals, providing also a secure attachment for the vertical members of the

A production 1500 Coupé, showing how the doors were slightly modified to accommodate wind-up windows and the modifications made to the rear pillar of the top to adapt it to production.

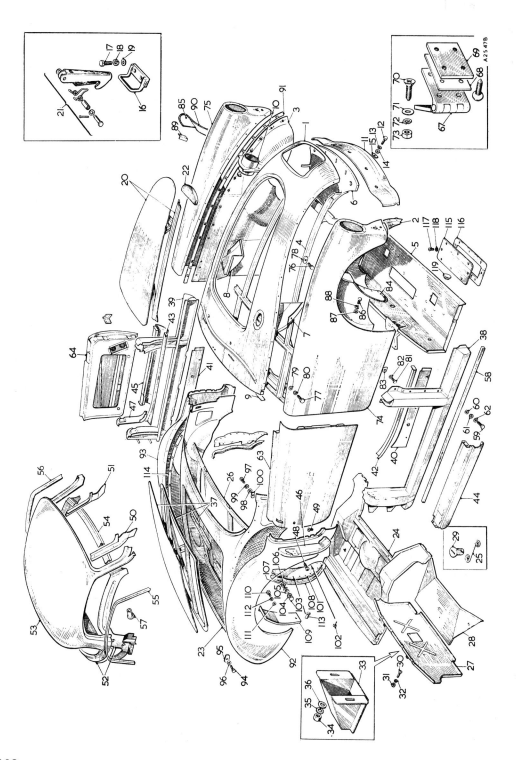

This exploded view from the MGA manual shows the components which went together to make up the coupé top, as well as illustrating the ultimate in the press tool designer's art, a one-piece pressing for the roof panel.

KEY TO THE BODY SHELL (COUPÉ)

No.	Description	No.	Description
1	Panel assembly – bonnet surround	60	Nut for bolt
2	Front side assembly – RH	61	Lock washer for nut
3	Front side assembly – LH	62	Washer – plain – for nut
4	Bonnet surround reinforcement	63	Door assembly – RH
5	Panel assembly – front bulkhead	64	Door assembly – LH
6	Panel – radiator duct	67	Hinge – door
7	Box assembly – RH air duct	68	Packing – door hinge
8	Box assembly – LH air duct	69	Plate – tapping
9	Strip – front bulkhead packing	70	Screw fixing hinge
10	Tube – air duct	71	Washer – plain – for screw
11	Panel – front valance	72	Washer – spring – for screw
12	Screw fixing panel	73	Nut for screw
13	Washer – spring – for screw	74	Wing assembly – RH front
14	Washer – plain – for screw	75	Wing assembly – LH front
15	Washer – plate – for screw	76	Screw – front wing to body
16	Bracket – bonnet lock safety catch	77	Screw – front wing to body
17	Screw fixing bracket	78	Washer – plate – for screw
18	Washer – spring – for screw	79	Washer – plain – for screw
19	Washer – plain – for screw	80	Washer – spring – for screw
20	Panel assembly – bonnet lid	81	Screw – front wing to sill
21	Catch assembly – safety	82	Washer – spring – for screw
22	Batten – bonnet lid stiffening	83	Washer – plate – for screw
23	Tonneau panel	84	Splash plate – RH front wing
24	Floor assembly – boot	85	Splash plate – LH front wing
25	Dzus spring	86	Screw fixing plate
26	Reinforcement assembly – tonneau	87	Washer – plain – for screw
27	Panel assembly – rear bulkhead	88	Washer – spring – for screw
28	Panel assembly – battery cover	89	Bracket assembly – splash plate
29	Dzus fastener	90	Seal – LH front splash plate (rubber)
30	Screw – rear bulkhead panel	91	Piping – front wing
31	Nut for screw	92	Wing assembly – RH rear
32	Washer – spring – for screw	93	Wing assembly – LH rear
33	Bracket assembly – spare wheel	94	Screw – rear wing to body
34	Nut for bracket	95	Washer – plate – for screw
35	Washer – spring – for nut	96	Washer – plain – for screw
36	Washer – plain – for nut	97	Screw – rear wing to sill
37	Lid assembly – boot	98	Washer – plain – for screw
38	Sill reinforcement and pillar assembly – RH	99	Washer – spring – for screw
39	Sill reinforcement and pillar assembly – LH	100	Washer – plate – for screw
40	Panel – sill inner – RH	101	Splash plate – rear wing – front – LH
41	Panel – sill inner – LH	102	Screw fixing plate
42	Plate – sill sealing – RH	103	Screw fixing plate
43	Plate – sill sealing – LH	104	Washer – plain – for screw
44	Panel – sill outer – RH	105	Washer – plain – for screw
45	Panel – sill outer – LH	106	Washer – spring – for screw
46	Panel – RH shut pillar facing	107	Nut for screw
47	Panel – LH shut pillar facing	108	Seal – RH rear splash plate (rubber)
48	Screw – facing panel – side	109	Splash plate – rear wing – rear – RH
49	Screw – facing panel – bottom	110	Screw fixing plate
50	Pillar reinforcement – windscreen – RH	111	Washer – plain – for screw
51	Pillar reinforcement – windscreen – LH	112	Washer – spring – for screw
52	Roof assembly	113	Rivet – rubber seal to plate
53	Panel assembly – roof	114	Piping – rear wing
54	Reinforcement assembly – roof panel	115	Cover-plate – heater aperture
55	Dripway – door opening – RH	116	Gasket – heater sealing
56	Dripway – door opening – LH	117	Screw – cover plate
57	Rivet – dripway to roof panel	118	Washer – spring – for screw
58	Finisher – sill lower	119	Grommet – blanking heater valve control hole
59	Bolt for sill finisher (special)		

channel section window frames, which were made from chrome-plated brass.

A chrome-plated upper door surround doubled as a rainwater gutter and made the door design of the coupé also look as much a part of the car as did the roof, again as though it belonged. The door sealing strip was a single piece, starting and ending at the bottom front corner of each door, mounted on the inner edge of the door surround. Two hinges hung each door, though there was only a single rubber buffer, whereas there were two on the roadster doors. The doors were now lockable, the driver's side being lockable from the outside on most cars, though on the very early examples, the key-operated lock (using the same key as operated the ignition) was on the left side, regardless of whether the car was left- or right-hand-drive.

The right-hand door, in the case of the early cars, but the passenger side door in every other case, was lockable only from the inside – inconvenient in some ways, but making it very difficult to lock the keys inside the car. The door handles were quite novel, in that they were mounted vertically and pulled downwards to open the doors. When the doors were closed, the open end of each handle rested on a small rubber buffer set into a socket in the end of the handle. That was fine until the buffer fell out and, with wear, the handles became loose and then chattered on the frame.

Inside the Coupé, trim was slightly more plush than on the roadster, the door panels being the first sign. Of necessity, they were now flat and carried door furniture (door handles and window winders) similar to all the other BMC 'B' Series cars, as well as a padded horizontally-ribbed panel covering what would have been the recess into the door lock pull-cords and map pockets of the roadster. Because the door pockets had now gone, two bin-type map pockets were fitted to the scuttle side panels to replace them. Other little trim variations included full-width transverse pleats on the seat squabs, without the longitudinal support rolls that were part of the open car's seats and which helped to keep the occupants in their places.

De Luxe seats, available on both roadster and coupé, had support rolls around both squabs and back-rests of driver and passenger seats. These were a very worthwhile option, as were the (as yet unfashionable) seat belts, as together they made for greater comfort and safety on long-distance runs in the MGA Coupé, which was available as 1500 and Twin-Cam, as well as the later 1600 and 1600 Mark II, versions. The Coupé became a highly successful design variant of the MGA, though it seems to have been most popular in 1500 form, selling just under 6,300, while the Twin-Cam version sold only 323 and the two versions of 1600 amassed just over 3,000 between them.

FIRST REACTIONS TO THE COUPÉ

Announced in September 1956, the original 1,500cc-engined version of the MGA Coupé was well received by press and public alike. As a specialist market vehicle, it was never going to sell by the tens of thousands, but orders soon came into Abingdon and by the end of 1957 over 4,000 had been built, 400 of which were retained in the home market. Just to put that into perspective, there were thirty more MGA Coupés sold in the home market in 1957 than MGA Roadsters, the vast bulk of production of both going to the United States and most of them to the West Coast. Similar numbers of left-hand-drive and right-hand-drive export models went to Europe and the Commonwealth (including South Africa).

Motor shows came and went and members of an enthusiastic public crawled all over the new coupé, admiring its well proportioned lines and in awe of the skill with which the top had been added to the MGA to make it look as though that had been the way it was designed from the start. But it was mid-1957 before the press managed to take possession of a coupé for long enough to conduct any form of review and *The Autocar* was first, in May. Their first impression was that the coupé was a worthy addition, being a wind-cheating and handsome body with a roof line that gave plenty of head-room without having the appearance of an ugly bubble.

It was noted that the mechanical specification of the MGA Coupé had been improved in the process of producing this new variant. Now it had more brake horsepower, 72, to pull it along and, with the benefit of aerodynamically cleaner lines, it had a better top speed, too, as well as improved fuel consumption. The power gain was only 4bhp but the cleaner lines helped the car make the best use of the small improvement to take it up to that magic 100mph top speed.

This was the first true volume production, 100mph British sports car of 1,500cc engine capacity. And what was more, the price wasn't *too* far out of reach at £699 (purchase tax taking the price up over £1,000 at that time), being just £104 more than the roadster. There are many who take the view, this author included, that the MGA Coupé truly restored the 'Magic' to MG, for not only did it take its driver to that 'magic' 100mph (just) in standard form, so 'clean' was it aerodynamically that its fuel consumption was markedly improved, too. It was easily possible, at realistic cruising speeds, to return over 30mpg (9.4l/100km) and on long runs this figure could rise even higher.

Having said so many pleasant things about the MGA Coupé, it might easily be concluded that it was that rare product of the British Motor Industry, the fault-free motor car! Not so, though it was a pretty good attempt. One major criticism of this coupé, as with many of its contemporaries, was that the doors didn't open wide enough to allow anyone who wasn't fit and slim (and equipped with almost double-jointed knees) to enter and leave the car easily. The angle of the door when fully open was little more than 45 degrees, so it was easy enough to

The MGA Coupé with wire wheels and optional badge bar on the front (many a one of those has saved an MGA radiator grille from mutilation).

MGA COUPÉ

CONDITIONS
Weather: Wind 10 to 15mph; showery. (Temperature 78°F, Barometer 29.6 in Hg). Surface: Concrete: Montlhery Track. Fuel: British and French Premium.

INSTRUMENTS
Speedometer at 30 mph	3% fast
Speedometer at 60 mph	3% fast
Speedometer at 90 mph	4% fast
Speedometer at 100 mph	7% fast
Distance recorder	accurate

WEIGHT
Kerb weight (unladen, but with oil, coolant and fuel for approx. 50 miles)	18½cwt
Front/rear distribution of kerb weight	52/48
Weight laden as tested	21¾ cwt

MAXIMUM SPEEDS
Flying Montlhéry lap	101.2 mph
Best one-way ½km time equals	103.8 mph

'Maximile' speed. (Timed quarter mile after one mile accelerating from rest.)
Mean of four runs	92.0 mph
Best one-way time equals	94.8 mph

Speed in Gears. at recommended limit of 5,500 rpm.
Max. speed in third	68 mph
Max. speed in second	42 mph
Max. speed in first	26 mph

FUEL CONSUMPTION
47.0 mpg at constant 40 mph on level
43.2 mpg at constant 50 mph on level
35.4 mpg at constant 60 mph on level
31.2 mpg at constant 70 mph on level
28.8 mpg at constant 80 mph on level
24.8 mpg at constant 90 mph on level

Overall Fuel Consumption for 742 miles, 26.9 gallons equals 27.6 mpg (10.2 litres/100 km)
Touring Fuel Consumption (mpg at steady speed midway between 30 mph and maximum, less 5% allowance for acceleration) 31.5 mpg
Fuel tank capacity (maker's figure) 10 gallons.

STEERING
Turning circle between kerbs:
Left	28½ feet
Right	29½ feet
Turns of steering wheel from lock to lock	2¾

ACCELERATION TIMES from standstill
0–30 mph	5.0 sec
0–40 mph	7.2 sec
0–50 mph	10.8 sec
0–60 mph	15.7 sec
0–70 mph	21.4 sec
0–80 mph	32.1 sec
Standing quarter mile	19.8 sec

ACCELERATION TIMES on upper ratios
	Top gear	3rd gear
10–30 mph	13.6 sec	8.1 sec
20–40 mph	13.6 sec	7.9 sec
30–50 mph	13.8 sec	8.1 sec
40–60 mph	12.6 sec	8.7 sec
50–70 mph	13.7 sec	10.4 sec
60–80 mph	17.6 sec	—
70–90 mph	28.1 sec	—

HILL CLIMBING at sustained steady speeds
Max gradient on top gear
1 in 10.7 (Tapley 210lb/ton)
Max gradient on 3rd gear
1 in 7.3 (Tapley 305lb/ton)
Max gradient on 2nd gear
1 in 4.75 (Tapley 472lb/ton)

BRAKES
0.94g retardation (equivalent to 32 ft. stopping distance) with 90 lb. pedal pressure.
0.80g retardation (equivalent to 37½ ft. stopping distance) with 75 lb. pedal pressure.
0.52g retardation (equivalent to 58 ft. stopping distance) with 50 lb. pedal pressure.
0.27g retardation (equivalent to 115 ft. stopping distance) with 25 lb. pedal pressure.

The Motor was once again one of the first to produce a road test of the new model and here are its findings.

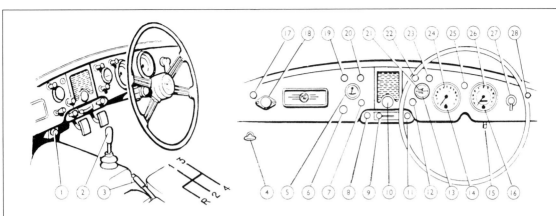

1, Headlamp dip switch. 2, Gear lever. 3, Handbrake. 4, Bonnet catch release. 5, Fuel contents gauge. 6, Windscreen washer control. 7, Choke control. 8, Ventilator control. 9, Temperature and heater fan switch. 10, Horn button. 11, Demisting control. 12, Starter button. 13, Water thermometer. 14, Dynamo charge warning light. 15, Trip re-setting knob. 16, Headlamp main beam indicator light. 17, Map reading light switch. 18, Map reading light. 19, Windscreen wipers switch. 20, Ignition switch. 21, Oil pressure gauge. 22, Lights switch. 23, Fog lamp switch. 24, Tachometer. 25, Panel light switch. 26, Speedometer and distance recorder. 27, Direction indicator switch. 28, Direction indicator warning light.

slide the left leg into place and then pull the body in after it to sit at the steering wheel. It was screwing up the right leg to slide the foot into the footwell, past the door pillar, that was the real problem. And a driver with a girth of greater than average found it that much more difficult.

Once in, the optional telescopic steering column made a minute contribution to achieving a comfortable driving position, but closing the door could well have been another matter. The bent wire 'garden gate-style' door pull was really a pretty flimsy device for closing a door which took a bit of effort if the windows were closed, as the back pressure was enough to resist anything like a light-to-reasonable pull. A hefty heave of the door could, on the other hand, result in the embarrassed driver sitting looking at a detached door pull in the palm of his or her hand. A clear case of needing to develop a technique!

The driver of an MGA in any form had to manipulate the left foot around the clutch pedal to reach the foot-operated dip switch while avoiding inadvertently disengaging

the clutch – all at anything up to 80mph (130km/h), which was pretty close to the limit of vision allowed by the headlights (the range of Lucas PL700 or contemporary Marchal headlamp inserts would have distinctly improved the view). Conversion of headlamps was carried out by the occasional owner determined to have better high-speed night vision. And more than one person in the past put forward the idea of a horn push in the middle of the steering column, with a hand-operated dip-switch in place of the existing horn push as a solution.

THE 1500 COUPÉ ON THE ROAD

Given that the MGA Coupé was said to be almost 210lb (95kg) heavier than the roadster, the extra 4bhp with which it was endowed was surely to be of little real benefit in improving the performance, except that the slight improvement in power improved the free-revving capacity of the engine, so giving a little help. But improved performance through cleaner lines was confirmed by the road testers when they finally managed to win possession of a car for long enough to put it through its paces.

In serious production for six months before *The Autocar* won its chance to stage a real challenge to the car's ability, the world at large was either thoroughly familiar with the general appeal of the car, or lived in somewhere like Siberia! Of course, we must also remember that this road test was conducted in the throes of a fuel shortage, post-Suez, so the availability of cars for such flippant activities as road testing was limited. Even so, it was decided to test the car in Britain, rather than following that magazine's normal practice of taking sports cars on to the Continent to check out their credentials.

In performance terms, the road tester found the car wanted for little, except perhaps that it took almost 2 miles (3.2km) to reach the car's maximum speed, which is not that much of a criticism when you realize that he was simply trying to prove that this car really was capable of 100mph (160km/h). The fact of the matter was that he, and most owners, would be perfectly satisfied with an optimum cruising speed of 80–85mph (130–137km/h), of which the car was capable with ease.

The 0–60mph time for the coupé was a second faster than the original roadster time, at 15 seconds. It was still not sparkling for a sports car, though there were the options of tuning and closer ratio gears described earlier in this volume. On the plus side, this was likely to be a car that would be driven a little less aggressively anyway, it was thought, as it wasn't the kind of car the old hair shirt sports car brigade would buy, they said. In fact, the coupé was probably subjected to every bit as rough treatment as was the roadster, because those who bought it were still MG fans. *The Autocar* managed a best of exactly 102mph (164km/h) from their test car, a fuel consumption of 25–35 mpg (9.4–11.3l/100km), but found a few things to criticize.

Among their criticisms were things like: the doors let in some draughts as the windows shook at high speeds and on poor surfaces; there were distortions in the corners of the windscreen, such as would cause the driver to have to look twice at times (not a happy situation at speed!); the horn push was in an inconvenient location (told you so!); the light switch wasn't in the easiest place to reach and the flashing direction indicator switch should have been on the steering column, not on the dashboard. All valid comments, but fortunately none serious enough to deter any but the pickiest of would-be owners.

Some of these faults were picked up again by other road testers, including 'WB' of *Motor Sport*, who also criticized the rear view mirror for its position. His cure was to '. . .throw it over the hedge and fit the wing mirror offered as an extra'. 'WB' found little to criticize about the curvature of the windscreen at its extremes, however, though he did regret the lack of a cubby-hole (chances are that if one had been provided, it would not have been big enough to accommodate *Motor Sport*'s editorial Rolleiflex anyway). There were a few other mild comments, like the fact that while a crash pad surrounded the scuttle rear edge, it would be unlikely to provide any real protection in the event of a head-on shunt.

All in all, 'WB' was well pleased with the handling and performance of the coupé, though he raised the same criticism about the gap between second and third gears as others had raised in reviews of the roadster. In this road test, which covered something approaching 1,000 miles (1,600km), fuel consumption was found to be around 27.5 mpg (10.3l/100km) on average, giving a range of 275 miles (442km) for the car between fill-ups at estimated worst. Driving a little more sedately might well have raised the range to 300 miles (485km), but no more than that. Oil consumption was the Achilles heel of the MGA in this road test, as several pints went

MG A COUPÉ

SPECIFICATIONS

List price	$2750
Wheelbase, in	94.0
Tread, f and r	47.4/48.8
Tire size	5.60–15
Curb weight, lb	2080
distribution, %	52/48
Test weight	2320
Engine	4 cly, ohv
Bore & stroke	2.875 x 3.5
Displacement, cu in	90.8
cc cm	1489
Compression ratio	8.30
Horsepower	72
peaking speed	5500
equivalent mph	94.7
Torque, lb-ft	77.4
peaking speed	3500
equivalent mph	60.3
Gear ratios, overall	
4th	4.30
3rd	5.91
2nd	9.52
1st	15.6

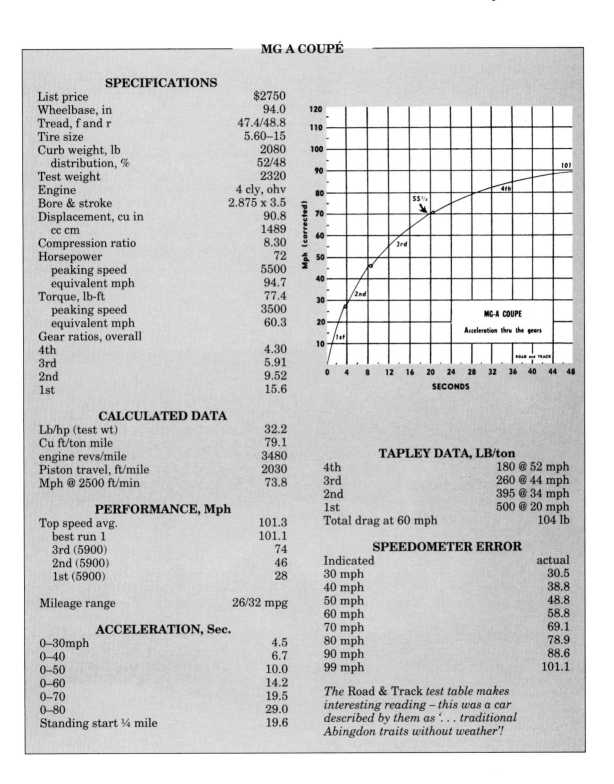

CALCULATED DATA

Lb/hp (test wt)	32.2
Cu ft/ton mile	79.1
engine revs/mile	3480
Piston travel, ft/mile	2030
Mph @ 2500 ft/min	73.8

PERFORMANCE, Mph

Top speed avg.	101.3
best run 1	101.1
3rd (5900)	74
2nd (5900)	46
1st (5900)	28
Mileage range	26/32 mpg

ACCELERATION, Sec.

0–30mph	4.5
0–40	6.7
0–50	10.0
0–60	14.2
0–70	19.5
0–80	29.0
Standing start ¼ mile	19.6

TAPLEY DATA, LB/ton

4th	180 @ 52 mph
3rd	260 @ 44 mph
2nd	395 @ 34 mph
1st	500 @ 20 mph
Total drag at 60 mph	104 lb

SPEEDOMETER ERROR

Indicated	actual
30 mph	30.5
40 mph	38.8
50 mph	48.8
60 mph	58.8
70 mph	69.1
80 mph	78.9
90 mph	88.6
99 mph	101.1

The Road & Track *test table makes interesting reading – this was a car described by them as '. . . traditional Abingdon traits without weather'!*

in during the run, calculated to produce an average consumption rate of 2,000mpg (0.14l/100km). Whilst higher oil consumptions in those days were commonplace, that seems pretty high, especially when one begins to get concerned at anything more than 1,000 miles per *pint* (0.035l/100km)in the 1990s.

In all the reviews conducted on the 1500 MGA Coupé, all thought the styling of the car was excellent, that in general terms the product quality was good and that there were few cars in the 1,500cc category which could equal the performance, the comfort, the economy and the price. Given that there weren't many cars being produced in that category anyway, strictly speaking, it was less of an accolade than the car truly deserved. The

mechanical specification of the car had really already been proven by that time, anyway, so it was much more a matter of how the road testers reacted to the confined space of a coupé version.

The reader would have expected a deeply analytical – and critical – road test from the pages of *Autosport*, as John Bolster had a reputation for being very direct in his appraisal of anything he road tested. The MGA was no exception to that rule and Mr Bolster did a thorough job. He was one of the first to observe the restricted access through the doors of the coupé, it being much less noticeable on the roadster, as the driver didn't have to stoop to miss the roof while getting in to that model, whereas the problem of contorting oneself at two angles of approach upon

The 1600 Coupé followed the 1500 and, apart from the badging looked little different.

The final version of the MGA Coupé was the 1600 Mark II, this elegant example belonging to Jonathan Stein, Publishing Director of Automobile Quarterly, *who lives in Reading, Pennsylvania. He is recognized as a leading expert in the United States on MGAs, especially the Coupé.*

entry to the coupé was much more demanding. Even so, once in, he really put the car through its paces. A demonstration of just how thorough Mr Bolster was is that he drove the same vehicle as was reviewed by *Autocar* and *Motor Sport* and managed to squeeze a 0–60 time of 14.2 seconds from it!

He also managed to push the car to 102.27mph (164.65km/h), while returning an average fuel consumption of only 26mph (10.9l/100km), though he did admit to driving the car hard (he must have done to achieve his quoted 0–60 time) and did point out that more sedate driving would produce a better return. *Motor* magazine, on the other hand, took the test car (still the same car – NJB381) to Montlhéry, France's answer to Brooklands, and in a temperature of 78°F (25.5°C) extracted 103.8mph (167.1km/h) on the banked track, but only 15.7 seconds for their standing-start 0–60mph test. Fuel consumption was little better than John Bolster's result, though they did put in fifty laps of Montlhéry as part of the test. The only notable criticism to come from this quarter was the limited arc of the windscreen wipers which, at high speed on the open road would be quite a valid point.

As you look inside the boot of this 1600 Mark II, you realize why the luggage rack was so popular, especially if you opted for the 5.90 tyre size and wire wheels. Soft bags inside the boot were almost essential.

The door handles on all Coupés were vertical, hinged from the bottom. This picture shows the handle on a 1600 Mark II Coupé. You will note that the upper end of the handle doesn't quite come into contact with the vertical door pillar. This is because the rubber buffer which should sit in a socket on the end of the door handle is missing. Its purpose was to eliminate chatter and damage to the chrome.

From any angle, the MGA Coupé was well proportioned: from this slightly overhead viewpoint, the car looks even more attractive.

THE TWIN-CAM ACQUIRES A ROOF

Shortly after the MGA Twin-Cam roadster was introduced, a coupé version was announced, making all the attributes of the Twin-Cam available in closed form for those who no longer wanted to endure large volumes of fresh air as part of their sporting motoring. It was inevitable that this option should follow, as the higher powered version would surely appeal in the North American market and so earn more dollar revenue. It was fortunate that no one at Abingdon was holding their breath waiting for the orders to come rushing in, for they didn't. Only forty-eight Twin-Cam Coupés were built in 1958, twenty-six of those being for the home

market – an unusually high number as a proportion of the total built, even though so few were made.

The year 1959 was not a lot better, though the market was now split by three models of MGA Coupé; the 1500, the Twin-Cam and the new 1600 Coupé which came on stream that year. Just over 840 1500s left the factory in 1959, 260-odd Twin-Cams and over 1,200 1600s, making the 1600 the most popular option. As a percentage of total model production, the Twin-Cam figures don't look quite so bad, for just over 17 per cent of Twin-Cams built that year were coupés, compared with 19 per cent of 1500s in 1957, the best year of production for that variant of the MGA.

Of course, the 1500 MGA went out of

A Twin-Cam Coupé going slightly more sideways than was ever intended, at Silverstone.

A nice rear quarter view of the Twin-Cam Coupé, showing that the perennial luggage rack was still considered an essential. The owner of this car was HRH Prince Michael of Kent, who was then serving in West Germany.

production in 1959 and, a year later the Twin-Cam followed it into oblivion, not least because of the warranty problems being encountered with the Twin-Cam, largely because oil consumption was horrifyingly high and owners didn't seem to want to check oil levels as regularly as they should, because the dipstick wasn't in a convenient enough place to be sure that they would. So, of course, the coupés followed the fates of their respective roadsters and went into demise, leaving the future of the most prolific MG sports car to the newer 1600 model, which took advantage of Appendix J of the FIA's capacity rules allowing 1,600cc to supplant 1,500cc in international competition.

8 Appendix 'J' and the MGA 1600

For 1959 Appendix 'J' of the FIA's International Sporting Code (the part of the Code which dealt with engine capacity classes), introduced changes to the old capacity limits across the board. Newer and narrower capacity bands were introduced and the old 1,100cc to 1,500cc Class 'F' was to disappear and be replaced by three new classes, one of 1,001cc to 1,150cc, another of 1,150cc to 1,300cc and the third from 1,301cc to 1,600cc. This meant that many car manufacturers would increase the engine capacity of their products to take advantage of the new limits for family cars, while at the same time providing better power outputs for their sporting models.

Appendix 'J' was a godsend to the British Motor Corporation and the MGA. Since the British Motor Corporation needed more power for its production cars at minimum cost, the obvious route to follow was to take advantage of those Appendix 'J' changes and increase engine capacity and even though that increase was only 100 cubic centimetres, its development would lead to improved performance potential for the ponderous Pininfarina-styled 'B' Series BMC saloon cars and would ultimately give an opportunity for a level of standardization between the 'B' saloons and the MGA, the only sports car in their catalogues to be affected by that rule change.

By late 1958 the anticipated downturn in sales of the 1500 MGA was beginning to be felt and since the Twin-Cam, while never expected to be produced in anything like such numbers as the 1500, was a sales dis-

appointment to Abingdon, the announcement of the Appendix 'J' changes seemed to come just in time and much was made of the corporation's prompt reaction to it in the development of the 1600 MGA to meet new market demands (or pick up flagging sales, whichever point of view you took).

TO BUILD A NEW MGA

In North America during the summer of 1958, MG dealers were beginning to become restless about the 1,500cc MGA, pointing out that its engine was being overtaken in power output by cars with smaller engines. It was beginning to prove less competitive in racing and the dealers were also concerned that the two leading contenders for what they saw as a market in decline for the MGA were both quite a bit more expensive. The Twin-Cam was already a 1,600cc engine so, they argued, why not use the bore and stroke of that engine in a pushrod unit for the MGA and use the price advantage to push back sales of the Alfa Romeo Giulietta and the Porsche 356?

The 1,588cc engine of the MGA Twin-Cam used an adaptation of the crankcase from the increased capacity 'B' Series BMC engine, as has already been explained. Because sales of the original 1,500cc MGA were slowing down in North America, those in high places began to ask how the situation could be reversed. Abingdon was now able to capitalize on the Appendix 'J' changes, using that lifeline to switch to the 1,588cc block and produce a pushrod 1,600cc MGA suitable for use in

116

This 1600 Roadster was built to North American market specification, hence the whitewall tyres. The slightly different sidelights can be seen, as can the new sidescreens, with sliding perspex instead of celluloid-panelled flaps.

competition, giving it more power and certainly a little more torque. The point had not escaped them, either, that if the 1,600cc pushrod development was a success, as it could hardly fail to be, it would give Abingdon an ideal opportunity to kill off the Twin-Cam, which was beginning to prove an expensive exercise.

THE SECOND GENERATION MGA ARRIVES

The summer of 1959 saw the unveiling of the MGA 1600 which, apart from being fitted with the 1,588cc pushrod engine, had a few

body detail changes, too. These changes were also incorporated into the Twin-Cam for the remainder of its production life. The body specification was universal: which engine went in which chassis/body assembly made little technical difference (and not much time difference on the assembly line either).

External detail changes for the 1600 included a revised tail-light assembly, in which the tail-lamp mounting was made larger, to accommodate the separate round orange flasher that was positioned above the tail-lamp. The side-lamp was now much bigger and was a combined side-lamp flasher unit, with a large orange flasher forming two thirds of the lens area. This improved the

Despite the angle of opening of the MGA doors, it seems ladies could still enter and emerge from the car with their modesty intact, provided, perhaps, they weren't too tall! This view also shows the difference between the 1600 tail lights and those of the 1500.

car's safety considerably, especially at night, as the original flashers were integral with the side- and tail-lamps, so were white at the front and red at the rear, whereas amber was now the flasher colour at the front and rear ends of the 1600 (except in the USA, of course).

Badging on the MGA 1600 was little different from the earlier model, with a radiator grille and badge at the front of the car identical to those of the 1500 and the Twin-Cam. The air vent badge was also the same though, as on the Twin-Cam, a small additional badge appeared behind the vent with the simple inscription '1600' on it. At the back, on the boot lid, was the same simple chrome badge 'MG' as the other two models sported with, again in the fashion of the Twin-Cam, the inscription '1600' positioned below the 'MG'.

Other trim changes which came with the MGA 1600 were more practical. For example, the detachable sidescreens were now rigid-framed, so allowing the use of sliding windows which brought better ventilation to the car when the hood was up and sidescreens fitted. The studs upon which the sidescreens were mounted were of the same size as those on the earlier 1500 model, but the knurled front retaining nut was made larger to provide better security for the sidescreens and to give the occupants a better purchase action on tightening, so as reduce the risk of the screens flapping when in place.

To provide the support essential to the slightly heavier sidescreens, equipped with sliding perspex windows, a larger knurled locknut was fitted to the doors of the 1600.

Side-lights on the 1600 were larger than on the 1500, to allow for the incorporation of the amber flashers within the lens, which occupied the bottom two thirds of the lens area.

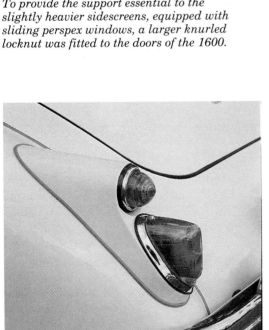

The 1600 tail lights in close-up.

Disc wheels remained standard on the MGA 1600, but now it had 11in disc brakes at the front to accompany the 10in rear drums of its predecessor. The standard hand-brake mechanism of the 1500 was also transferred to the 1600. Interestingly, some road tests of the time quote Dunlop disc brakes for the new 1600, while others say it was fitted with Lockheeds. There's no tangible evidence that any production 1600 was fitted with anything but Lockheeds, so it seems some pressmen assumed that since the Twin-Cam was fitted with Dunlops, it was fair to assume that the 1600 had the same, which was not correct.

The road wheels used on the 1600 were of a type already proven on its predecessor, the MGA 1500. The decision to retain disc wheels

The rear end of the 1600 showing the boot-mounted 'MG' badge and '1600'.

was based on the twin considerations of cost and unsprung weight, disc wheels being so much less expensive to produce than wires and so much lighter. The design advances being made in the field of car road wheels, as well as in the tooling for their manufacture, meant that disc wheels were becoming ever lighter and more resilient. Disc wheels needed less maintenance than wires and the hubs were also much lighter and less expensive to manufacture.

One of the developments in the MGA wheel was the addition of small pressed stiffeners in the central area of the nave,

adjacent to the retaining stud holes. This made the wheel much more rigid at the centre, while the thinner material of the disc part of the wheel (the nave) helped to make it lighter. As with the 1500 model it succeeded. The tyres remained 5.60 × 15, unlike the Twin-Cam, which had gone up to 5.90 × 15s from the outset. Some people queried the fact that the Twin-Cam had the same sized engine as the new 1600, yet larger tyres, but the factory response was the predictable one – that the Twin-Cam had so much more power and torque to put down, it needed a larger section tyre. A reasonable response, certainly, but the fact is that Abingdon needed to keep the price differential between the MGA 1500 and its successor to a minimum. Keeping disc wheels and 5.60-section tyres in the specification were just two ways of doing that without incurring major adverse market reactions.

There was another consideration, too, in the decision to develop the stud mounted disc wheel, both for the MGA and other sports cars built in Britain and elsewhere. This is because in the last months of the 1950s, there was already the seed of a safety campaign to outlaw the eared centre-lock wheel nut – the 'knock-off' nut. Campaigners in certain quarters were trying to build their case on the potential damage a 'knock-off' wheel nut could do in an accident, acting like the hubs of Boadicea's chariot to cut a swath through anything in its path.

Whether you support that view or not, it did ultimately gain credibility and so the ears disappeared from the 'knock-off', leaving a hexagonal nut that demanded a spanner for removal and installation. This slower process of wheel fitment and removal reduced the popularity of the centre-lock wheel, enhancing the opportunity for car makers to retain disc wheels and hold down their production costs. Cast alloy wheels

---

MGA 1600 Mark I

VEHICLE CONSTRUCTION

Rectangular-section steel-tube chassis with fabricated scuttle 'bridge' and pressed steel body structure with pressed steel panels

ENGINE

Crankcase/cylinder block	One piece cast iron
Cylinder head	Cast iron ohv
Cylinders	4
Compression ratio	8.3:1 standard (others optional)
Cooling system	Pressurized, thermo-syphon and pump
Bore and stroke	75.39 x 89mm
Engine capacity	1,588cc
Main bearings	Three shell-type
Valves	Single camshaft ohv pushrod/rocker
Fuel supply method and type	SU high pressure electric pump
Quoted max. power	79.5bhp @ 5,600rpm
Quoted max. torque	87lb/ft @ 3,800rpm

BRAKES

Type	Lockheed disc brakes front, drum brakes rear
Size	11in front discs; 10 x 1¾in drum rear

TRANSMISSION

Clutch type	Single dry plate Borg & Beck A6G
Gearbox ratios	2R, 0.468:1; 1, 15.652:1; 2, 9.520:1; 3, 5.908:1; 4, 4.300:1; standard
Final drive ratio	Hypoid bevel 4.300:1 standard

SUSPENSION AND STEERING

Front suspension	Independent coil/piston dampers
Rear suspension	Semi-elliptic/piston dampers
Steering type	Rack and pinion, 2.66 turns
Wheel type and size	Vented disc 4J x 15in stud mounted
Tyre size and rating	5.60 x 15in

VEHICLE DIMENSIONS (in/mm)

Overall length	156/3,962
Overall width	58/1,473
Wheelbase	94/2,388
Track	
front	47.5/1,206
rear	48.75/1,238
Overall height	50/1,270

would ultimately take the place of the centre-lock in mass-market fashion accessories for sports cars. Before many more years had passed, only sports racing cars would use centre-lock wheels, where air-operated tools were used for their installation and removal, to keep pit-stop times to a minimum. In the middle 1990s, even the most exotic of road-going sports cars, Aston Martins and Ferraris among them, use cast alloy stud-mounted wheels. The centre-lock with eared nut is a relic of a lost age.

THE 1600 POWERHOUSE

The powerhouse for the MGA 1600 was a larger-bore version of the existing 1,500cc cylinder block, retaining the stroke of that unit, though that is not the whole story. In January 1959 a modified version of the 1500 engine's cylinder block was introduced, the 15GD variant. The starter motor was in a higher position than on the earlier 15GB type, which required a modified bell housing for the gearbox, a differently shaped right-hand toeboard and a cover over the Bendix drive of the starter. The carpet was also modified to accommodate the changes. The hole for a mechanical fuel pump, which was never used on any MGA engine, was no longer machined into the block and then blanked off, though the mounting face was still cast into the block.

With changes being made to the cylinder block/crankcase casting, it was decided also to incorporate the facility to cast in the nominal engine capacity, as on the 1500, with the digits '1500' appearing on the rear end of the right face of the block, just below the change in section where the cylinder block ends and the crankcase begins. The 1600 was on the drawing-board as these minor casting changes were being made, so as the 1,600cc engine went into production in May 1959, so the digits '1600' were cast into the

block for that variant of the BMC 'B' Series engine.

The bore of the 'new' 1600 (remember the Twin-Cam had been a 1600 from its inception, so a 1600 MGA had been available for just over a year) was the same as that for the Twin-Cam at 75.41mm, whilst the stroke remained 89mm, giving an actual engine capacity of 1,588cc, just under the new Class Limit of Appendix 'J' and allowing enough latitude for re-boring of the engine in service while keeping it below the 1,600cc limit. There had been no problems with cylinder block cooling on the Twin-Cam engine, so that bore was considered to have been well proven in service and pistons to that bore were already in manufacture, so there was little pattern work to be undertaken for the casting of pistons, thus the development costs were held down in that area.

Another area where development costs were held down was in the cylinder head for the 1600, because this was identical to the one used on the 1500 from the introduction of the MGA, even to the extent of retaining the '1500' type identifier cast into it. In the eyes of some, this was a retrograde step, as it had been thought that Abingdon would have taken the chance to modify the head along the lines of the very successful Derrington cylinder head offered for the earlier version. It was almost certainly the power-base at Longbridge who prevented the creation of a new cylinder head for the 1600, as it was such a small volume demand in the total BMC 'B' Series engine production.

There is no doubt that, had Longbridge wanted to, they could have supplied Abingdon with 'short' engines (lacking a cylinder head and valve gear), with the valve operating components supplied loose. This would have allowed Abingdon to do a deal with a specialist supplier, such as Derringtons, to fit a full eight-port cross-flow cylinder head that would allow the engine to breathe, instead of stifling much of the extra potential with the old

Engine room of the 1600.

five-port type with its siamesed inlets and worse, one siamesed and two individual exhaust ports – an absolute tuner's nightmare.

Siamesed porting has never met with favour among engine tuners, not only because of gas flow routing, but more significantly, the facility to enlarge the port sizes is restricted. Most tuners have managed to cope with that where there are two pairs of siamesed ports in a four-cylinder engine, because it has usually been on the inlet side and one carburettor to two cylinders can be made to work quite well. However, in developing the extraction characteristics of an exhaust system, siamesing the ports to the inner pair of cylinders creates more problems, as the control and equalization of gas flows and pressures is inhibited by the very design concept of directing four into three. The only excuse for using the five-port head on the MGA was manufacturing cost.

That this comment is true is borne out by the market growth in Derrington, and others, producing four-inlet-port (though still three exhaust) cylinder heads to replace the original five-port. What is more, the significant performance improvements are not just testament to the success of these aftermarket products, they are damning of the original design, for the simple replacement of a cylinder head, without change to valve or ignition timing, compression ratio or carburettor needles, resulted in substantial power improvement.

Standard compression ratio of the new engine was retained at 8.3:1, as it had been on the 1500. Valve timing was also the same at 16/50/51/21 degrees, though rocker clearances were reduced from 0.017in to 0.015in. The valves themselves were of the same size as on the 1500 and most of the rest of the engine specification remained common, though the piston ring clearances for the oil control ring were slightly increased. Clearly, the transition from 1500 MGA to 1600 MGA was to be at the lowest possible cost.

THE NEW ENGINE ON THE ROAD

The motoring world received the new MGA 1600 with enthusiasm, little thought being given to the Twin-Cam in the process of greeting the new model as the logical development of the original MGA. Of course it *was* the logical development of the 1500 and MG's Abingdon factory was certainly not going to spoil its introduction with oblique references to the potential of the (1600) Twin-Cam either, since it was a car they saw the opportunity to kill off just as soon as the pushrod 1600 was established. The warranty costs of the Twin-Cam were mounting (much of that,

in hindsight, down to inept handling of Twin-Cams by inexperienced owners), but MG stuck to its long-established principle of putting customer satisfaction above any views it may have had about the way they might be treating their cars.

Abingdon's prime concern with the introduction of the 1600 was to restore the fallback in sales of the MGA and provide a car with slightly fewer gear changes per trip. The task before them, especially in overseas markets, was to persuade the would-be sports car buyer that a car such as the MGA 1600, with its sports car charisma and four-speed manual gearbox, would not be so much harder to drive than their larger-engined automatic-transmissioned family car. Torque was, of course, all-important in the process of transition to sports car driving. In this area, the MGA 1600 scored well, the extra 99cc endowing the car with an extra 9.6lbft (1.3kgm) for an additional 300rpm.

Brake horsepower in the 1600 was also up, though only by 7½bhp for an extra 100 rpm. This wasn't seen as being quite so important, however, in the process of creating a car that was easier to drive for the person more familiar with automatic-transmissioned low-stressed American cars. It was important, you see, to keep the enthusiasts convinced that this was still a hairy sports car which made no concessions to market forces, while the manufacturer actually widened the market appeal of the MGA 1600. The car's acceleration was more important than top speed and with almost two seconds lopped off the 0–60mph time, the corresponding improvement in acceleration in a high gear was what would ultimately convince the aspiring sports car driver that it perhaps wasn't so much harder to handle than the family Ford, Chevrolet or Holden.

Road manners were, of course, the next element in the formula. The handling of the MGA was already highly regarded, but the 10 per cent improvement in power and the

12 per cent improvement in torque would combine to help the car haul itself out of most situations. Gearing was also a major part of the MGA's formula for success and the 1600 enjoyed the same basic gearing as the 1500, with the same optional closer ratios and higher final drive available at extra cost to the buyer who could afford that luxury. At least, though, that luxury was one way of convincing the die-hard enthusiasts that the MGA was still a sports car to be reckoned with and one which was very economically priced against its market adversaries.

Driving the 1600 gave the novice driver a sense of confidence that was not so apparent in the 1500, simply as the result of increased torque and the consequent ability to hold the car in a given gear for longer on a bend, or to accelerate in a particular gear without having to change down. Fuel consumption on the road was reckoned to be down by around 4mpg, from about 28mpg (10.1l/100km) for the 1500 to just over 24 with the 1600. As has already been said, the top speed of the 1600 was about the same as the 1500, so if higher top speed was your quest, then this wasn't the car for you, but if sheer gutsy handling and an ability to get from point 'A' to point 'B' quicker than most was what you wanted, then this was your car.

DEVELOPING THE PERFORMANCE POTENTIAL

There was a lot of disappointment among MG sports cars enthusiasts that the company had not done more to improve the breathing of the MGA's engine with the introduction of the 1600. What many were blind to was the fact that the British Motor Corporation used thousands and thousands of 'B' Series engines in a very wide range of vehicles and so did not want to become involved in low-volume special options at a time when standardization was the all-

important goal of manufacturing industry. After all, standardization was the means of gaining higher production volumes and the creation of a special line for MG engines was less viable by the year. It was to be a few years yet before the 'special vehicle option' (a phrase coined and exploited by Ford) fashion would accommodate this kind of variation in manufactured specification.

MG, indeed BMC, was not the only manufacturing group to take the view that the best way to meet the needs of those wanting to make their cars perform was to sell conversion kits for specialists to install. This was to continue to be the way ahead for the enthusiast who wanted to exploit the performance potential of his MGA 1600, unless he wanted to invest the extra £300-odd in a Twin-Cam. But that was a 25 per cent hike in price for a car that was acquiring a reputation for being temperamental, and for less than that £300 the new 1600 owner could probably endow his pushrod-engined car with quite similar performance. After all, there were the factory-approved performance kits or, if you wanted better breathing, higher performance, improved fuel consumption and a lift in torque, then the Derrington cylinder head was now available for the 1600 – and it was to sell like the proverbial hot cakes.

The Abingdon-approved special tuning kits for the MGA 1600 provided five stages of tune, beginning with the same simple Stage One of polished ports and cylinder head as applied to the 1500. This yielded an extra 3bhp, whilst Stage Two reverted to the use of the Riley One-Point-Five camshaft and could be used in conjunction with Stage One to produce an additional 6bhp over the standard power output. Stage Three brought 9.25:1 compression ratio pistons into the formula. This, combined with the Stage 3A recommendation of 1¾in SU carburettors, using KW needles, brought 88bhp at 6,000rpm. Stage Five saw the use of the larger carburettors from Stage 3A combined

MG-JUDSON

SPECIFICATIONS

Price (kit only)	$2160
Wheelbase, in	94.0
Tread, f and r	47.4/48.8
Tire size, mm	165–380
Curb weight, lb	2110
distribution, %	52/48
Test weight	2390
Engine	4 cly, ohv
Bore & stroke	2.875 x 3.5
Displacement, cu in	90.8
cu cm	1489
Compression ratio	8.30
Horsepower (est.)	90
peaking speed	5500
equivalent mph	97.1
Torque, lb-ft (est).	95
peaking speed	3500
equivalent mph	61.8
Gear ratios, overall	
4th	4.30
3rd	5.91
2nd	9.52
1st	15.6

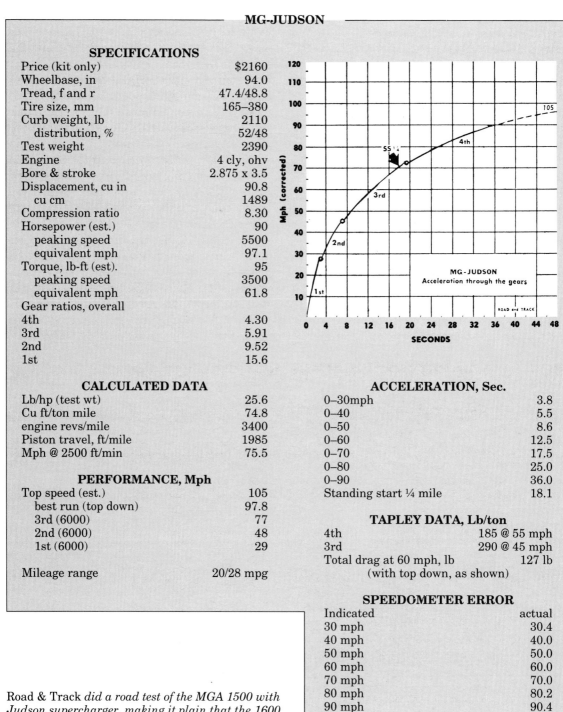

MG-JUDSON
Acceleration through the gears

ROAD and TRACK

CALCULATED DATA

Lb/hp (test wt)	25.6
Cu ft/ton mile	74.8
engine revs/mile	3400
Piston travel, ft/mile	1985
Mph @ 2500 ft/min	75.5

PERFORMANCE, Mph

Top speed (est.)	105
best run (top down)	97.8
3rd (6000)	77
2nd (6000)	48
1st (6000)	29
Mileage range	20/28 mpg

ACCELERATION, Sec.

0–30mph	3.8
0–40	5.5
0–50	8.6
0–60	12.5
0–70	17.5
0–80	25.0
0–90	36.0
Standing start ¼ mile	18.1

TAPLEY DATA, Lb/ton

4th	185 @ 55 mph
3rd	290 @ 45 mph
Total drag at 60 mph, lb	127 lb
(with top down, as shown)	

SPEEDOMETER ERROR

Indicated	actual
30 mph	30.4
40 mph	40.0
50 mph	50.0
60 mph	60.0
70 mph	70.0
80 mph	80.2
90 mph	90.4

Road & Track *did a road test of the MGA 1500 with Judson supercharger, making it plain that the 1600 would perform at least as well and so substantially better than the normally aspirated version.*

with re-shaped combustion chambers and planed cylinder head, as well as Type XF needles in the carburettors instead of the KWs of Stage 3A. Larger inlet and exhaust valves were also available and the ignition timing was set at 8 degrees BTDC. This level of tune was recommended for competition use only, though it was reckoned that 94bhp was the result.

By the time Stage Three was available for the 1600, Performance Equipment Company (PECO) in Great Britain and Judson in the United States both offered superchargers as the means of improving performance, though the Judson was still only really intended for the 1500. The attraction of this option was that it demanded no dismantling and reassembly of the engine other than the removal of the carburettors, the bolting-on of a pulley and the attachment of the super-

charger, with one carburettor, to the standard inlet manifold. The consequence of these quite minor labours, which left the basic engine in completely standard form, was an increase in brake horsepower and torque of around 25 per cent, according to Judson. The performance figures are much more interesting than the claimed power levels, though, as this is what the driver is interested in. In Britain, the Peco was said to give a 0–60mph time of 11.2 seconds, combined with an improvement in fuel consumption of around 10 per cent. The American version gave a 12.3-second 0–60 time, with little change to fuel consumption claimed. On the exchange rates of the day, there was little in the price of either conversion, the Peco costing just over £100 in Britain, while the Judson kit was priced at $260. The installation time and cost had to

On the track, the 1600 shows its road holding to good advantage, one being seen here driven by W.A. George at Silverstone.

be added in each case. Neither of these 'bolt-on' performance kits gave much extra in top speed, but the great value of both was that they seemed to do no damage to the engines upon which they were installed, whilst conferring a substantial performance gain in the lower to middle speed range of the car. Boost was around 5–6lb/in² (0.35–0.42kg/cm²) for both units and their removal was possible without leaving a trace of their ever having been installed.

The HRG-Derrington kit remained the most popular performance improvement choice in Britain, though there was still suspicion about the use of superchargers. Supercharging was still linked in the minds of many with the racing brutes of pre-war days and insurance companies did nothing to dispel the illusion with extra premiums for modified engines. The Derrington-HRG alloy cylinder head seemed to offer improvement in engine breathing, with a resultant improvement in fuel consumption, that seemed to make it worthwhile – and the conversion kit was certainly good value for money in over-the-counter price terms, costing just over £200 for the total package, including a pair of Weber 40DCOE carburettors.

Even without the Weber carburettors, using the Derrington-HRG head, leaving everything else on the engine standard, produced improvement that was little short of staggering. Power was increased to over 90bhp and torque to 85lb/ft (11.8kg/m), while with the full works, power rose to a very respectable 100bhp-plus, while torque came very close to 100lb/ft (13.8kg/m). This compared very well with the Twin-Cam, for a lot less money and, one suspects, a lot less heartache. But now, it was the turn of the press to make their judgement . . .

9 The MGA 1600's Reception and the De Luxe Model

Announced to the world in the summer of 1959, the first cars came together at Abingdon in May. The first road test of the MGA 1600 was a combination affair, set up by the British Motor Corporation to introduce the press to the new MGA and to the Austin Healey 3000, which was being put on sale at around the same time, having been announced just ahead of the MG model.

A TRIP THROUGH THE ALPS

Organized by the British Motor Corporation's press team, a trip to the south of France was reckoned to be an excellent way to introduce the press to the two new sports cars in its range. So six MGA 1600s and six Austin Healey 3000s were assembled at Lyon for a drive of around 300 miles (480km) to Cap d'Antibes, near Cannes. The intention was to complete the journey in a day, so demonstrating the ruggedness and performance potential of both cars. Then there would be three more days of driving around the south of France before the journalists returned home to write up their reports on the cars and the routes they took.

Motor Sport was one of the participants in this 'fun run' and their reporter wrote of meeting up on a cold and wet June morning (you know the kind of thing – the start of a typical British summer's day) at the Royal Automobile Club in Pall Mall, in central London, to be transported by coach to

Gatwick airport (in the days before half a million passengers a day went through it!) where they transferred to a Vickers Viscount (remember the world's first turbo-prop airliner?) to travel in silent comfort to Lyon. One has to presume that the use of the word 'silent' in this context was a relative statement, comparing the noise level with something like that of a Dakota or a Bristol Freighter, where decibel meters would have cracked under the strain, for the Viscount was not the quietest of airliners.

Arriving in the still relatively early morning, the team of intrepid British journalists was confronted with the twelve cars and the recommended route to Cap d'Antibes. This went from Lyon to Grenoble, then to Gap, on to Digne and Grasse, using the N85 and avoiding the N7 Autoroute, aiming to arrive at Cap d'Antibes in time for dinner and a restful evening, during which the individual merits of the two cars would be discussed into the early hours of morning, no doubt.

Because of the timing of the first day's events, the *Motor Sport* and *Autosport* correspondents decided to team up, 'MLT' of *Motor Sport* taking an MGA and Gregor Grant of *Autosport* taking a Healey. These two decided that a large chunk of the journey would be covered in darkness if they took the BMC recommended route, that there would still be a fair bit of country road to cover if they did take the N7 and that they would be in Cap d'Antibes at a half-reasonable hour by following their own route. So that was what they did. In the process, it gave our two journalists a chance to achieve a better comparison of the two cars' performances, relative to each other, than they might have had by taking the BMC route.

On the N7, the MGA 1600 was found to be remarkably fleet of foot, being able to keep the big 3-litre Healey in sight, despite the latter car's much bigger engine and consequent extra power. The controls of the MGA were found to be light and gear changes quick and smooth. Driving first to Montelimar (sampling the famous *nougat* en route), they next stopped at Avignon to fill up the cars and take refreshment themselves. The route from Aix-en-Provence to Cannes involved some pretty rough roads, with quite enough mountain corners to test the mettle of cars and drivers. Here was where the MGA shone, easily outperforming the Austin Healey, where power and straight line speed were of no help to it.

Over the remaining two days of the programme, journalists swapped cars and compared their new charges with the original ones. At this stage, the Healey was found to be a more ponderous vehicle to handle, rather heavier at the controls than the MGA and slower in the gear changes (it had a different and bigger gearbox to handle the higher power and torque). However, the extra power enabled the bigger car to be thrown about with a little more confidence, as the power was able to drag it out of slides in an almost casual manner, whereas there was a little more work in it for the MGA, which was running at higher engine speeds for the same result.

At the end of the four-day programme, which was only intended to be a press launch of the cars and not any kind of formal road test opportunity, the vehicles, which were all left-hand-drive and French-registered, were handed back to BMC to be delivered on to the Paris distributor, who would now sell them on as works demonstrators – and probably make more money as a consequence! The journalists climbed aboard an Air France scheduled flight from Nice, leaving behind the boredom of Riviera sunshine and water-skiing to go home and write up their reports. All found both cars a delight to drive and had little to say in criticism, though most found the MGA 1600 the more nimble of the two, as you might expect. The additional elbow room of the big Healey did find general favour, though most had something to say about the slightly awkward and stiff gear-change of the bigger car, favouring the smoother characteristics of the MGA.

FIRST REACTIONS FROM THE BRITISH PRESS

By September several journalists in Britain had sampled the delights of the 1600 MGA and were beginning to express their views. The performance of the 1600 was certainly better than that of the 1500, but was still not a serious match for a well-maintained Twin-Cam in good tune. However, the handling was thought to be considerably enhanced by the addition of the front disc brakes, improving the sense of confidence as a driver took his car close to its performance limits.

Particular performance improvements noted by *The Motor* included a top speed which just nudged 100mph, though the mean maximum in their test didn't quite make the 'ton', settling at 97.1mph (156.3km/h). On the other hand, the 0–60mph time clipped a good two seconds off the standard 1500 time, at 13.3 seconds. Braking, on the other hand, showed a near 10 per cent improvement from 30mph (48km/h), the stopping distance with the 1600's disc front brakes being just 30 feet (9.1m), as against just over 32½ feet (9.9m) with the drum brakes of the 1500.

Out on the open road, the correspondent found the 1600 a notable improvement on its predecessor, especially since the price of the

Richard Ide and P.J. McNally vie with each other for position in a relay race at Silverstone, Ide aboard a 1600 MGA.

new model was the same as the model it replaced. Since no fundamental changes had been made to the suspension of the MGA, or the steering, the front brakes and the extra power were what made this car different and better. The trim changes already described were noted by the tester, but the marginal reduction in unsprung weight at the front, resulting from disc brakes replacing drums (the actual weight differential between the two types of brakes was really quite small) and the slightly lighter road wheels, seems to have made a big enough difference in the handling to write about. Certainly, a bit more power in the middle range, combined

with a better ability to control it on brakes which had much less risk of fade, gave this car, in the eyes of *The Motor* correspondent, an excellent chance of recovering those lost sales of the 1500 MGA.

THE PRESS ROLLS ON

The Autocar had similar pleasing comments to make about the new 1600, though it was a little critical of the higher fuel consumption which came with just 99cc more engine capacity. Their recorded average consumption was just over 24mpg (11.8l/100km),

MG A 1600

CONDITIONS

Weather: Warm and dry, gusty 10 mph cross wind. (Temperature 59°F–63°F, Barometer 29.6–29.7 in Hg) Surface: Dry tar macadam and concrete. Fuel: Premium grade pump petrol (approx. 96 Research Method Octane rating).

INSTRUMENTS

Speedometer at 30 mph	accurate
Speedometer at 60 mph	3% fast
Speedometer at 90 mph	4% fast
Distance recorder	accurate

WEIGHT

Kerb weight (unladen, but with oil, coolant and fuel for approx. 50 miles)	18¼cwt
Front/rear distribution of kerb weight	53/47
Weight laden as tested	22 cwt

MAXIMUM SPEEDS

Flying lap of Banked Circuit	96.1 mph
Best one-way ¼ mile on straight	100 mph

'Maximile' speed. (Timed quarter mile after one mile accelerating from rest.)

Mean of four opposite runs	94.1 mph
Best ¼ mile time equals	96.3 mph

Speed in Gears. (at 6,000 rpm recommended limit).

Max. speed in 3rd gear	74 mph
Max. speed in 2nd gear	46 mph
Max. speed in 1st gear	28 mph

FUEL CONSUMPTION

39½ mpg at constant 30 mph on level
37 mpg at constant 40 mph on level
34½ mpg at constant 50 mph on level
32 mpg at constant 60 mph on level
29½ mpg at constant 70 mph on level
27 mpg at constant 80 mph on level
23 mpg at constant 90 mph on level

Overall Fuel Consumption for 1,028 miles, 42.2 gallons equals 24.4 mpg (11.6 litres/100 km)
Touring Fuel Consumption (mpg at steady speed midway between 30 mph and maximum, less 5% allowance for acceleration) 29.7 mpg

Fuel tank capacity (maker's figure) 10 gallons.

STEERING

Turning circle between kerbs:	
Left	29½ feet
Right	28½ feet
Turns of steering wheel from lock to lock	2¾

ACCELERATION TIMES from standstill

0–30 mph	4.3 sec
0–40 mph	6.4 sec
0–50 mph	9.1 sec
0–60 mph	13.3 sec
0–70 mph	17.7 sec
0–80 mph	25.1 sec
Standing quarter mile	19.8 sec

ACCELERATION TIMES on upper ratios

	Top gear	3rd gear
10–30 mph	12.1 sec	8.0 sec
20–40 mph	11.0 sec	6.9 sec
30–50 mph	10.6 sec	6.8 sec
40–60 mph	11.2 sec	7.4 sec
50–70 mph	13.3 sec	9.0 sec
60–80 mph	15.0 sec	—

HILL CLIMBING at sustained steady speeds

Max gradient on top gear	1 in 10.9 (Tapley 205lb/ton)
Max gradient on 3rd gear	1 in 7.3 (Tapley 305lb/ton)
Max gradient on 2nd gear	1 in 4.5 (Tapley 485lb/ton)

BRAKES

1.00g retardation (equivalent to 30 ft. stopping distance) with 100 lb. pedal pressure.
0.82g retardation (equivalent to 37¾ ft. stopping distance) with 75 lb. pedal pressure.
0.53g retardation (equivalent to 56¾ ft. stopping distance) with 50 lb. pedal pressure.
0.29g retardation (equivalent to 104 ft. stopping distance) with 25 lb. pedal pressure.

The Motor *still had trouble getting 100mph (160km/h) out of even the 1600 MGA and only managed it on its best one-way quarter mile.*

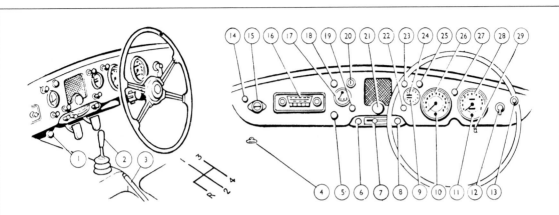

1, Headlamp dip switch. 2, Gear lever. 3, Handbrake. 4, Bonnet catch release. 5, Windscreen washer button. 6, Heater air-intake control. 7, Heater temperature control. 8, Demister control. 9, Water thermometer. 10, Dynamo charge warning light. 11, Headlamp main beam indicator lamp. 12, Direction indicator switch. 13, Direction indicator warning light. 14, Map-reading light switch. 15, Map-reading light. 16, Radio controls. 17, Fuel contents gauge. 18, Windscreen wipers. 19, Choke control. 20, Ignition switch. 21, Horn button. 22, Starter button. 23, Lights switch. 24, Oil pressure gauge. 25, Switch for optional fog-lamp. 26, Tachometer. 27, Panel light rheostat. 28, Speedometer and distance recorder. 29, Trip adjuster.

compared with over 28mpg (10.1l/100km) for the 1500. They did, however, go on to say that the average fuel consumption ought to be between 24 and 31mpg (11.8 and 9.1l/100km), which suggests that the car they had for road test was either somewhat out of tune or that its tester had a pretty heavy right foot – though the test report generally doesn't suggest that to be the case.

This reporter was generous, though, in his comments about the value of the power increase which came with the enlarged engine. The improvement in power and torque delivered very pleasing acceleration figures throughout the range – but most particularly in top gear at higher cruising speeds, the very performance area intended to appeal to the North American buyer, who would be used to the larger, ponderous vehicles indigenous to that continent as everyday transport.

Points to criticize were the louder exhaust note of the 1600, the apparent roughness of running when the engine speed of the test car reached 5,000rpm, causing the driver to have

to either accelerate out of the rough patch or decelerate to a speed well below it. Since there was little point in having a sports car if you were only going to drive it in top at speeds below 4,000rpm (just over 68mph (109km/h)!), the obvious thing to do was accelerate out of the vibration frequency. All that said, the tester confirmed that the car ran well at 80mph (130km/h), the optimum cruise speed of the car and a speed which would bring about an engine speed of just below 4,700rpm.

It would appear the *Autocar* test car could have done with a better pre-delivery check, as it seems, from reading the test report, that it was a bit of a 'lemon': consider the engine roughness (which was not typical of all 1600 MGAs), the fuel consumption and the particular point the tester made about the stiffness of the gearbox. It seems that at times, it required both hands to engage reverse gear, though the selector mechanism freed off during the test, so that it was showing positive signs of becoming a pleasant gearbox to work as the car was run in. The clutch, on the

The MGA 1600 from the rear quarter.

other hand was thought to be extremely good, being able to sustain sharp acceleration from a standstill and being smooth in operation under all test conditions.

Detail criticisms of the 1600 came in the areas of suspension, road shocks through the steering, sidescreens, interior space (a comment carried over from the review of the original MGA), location of the horn button, headlamps and dipswitch, and wind noise at speed. The suspension was thought to be a little on the firm side by the standards of the day, though the road shocks which came through the steering wheel were really a testament to the precision of the steering, not a fault. The same old complaints were raised about the fit of the sidescreens, the location of the horn button and the awkwardness of the headlamp dipswitch, to say nothing of the brilliance of the headlamps (which really were not as good as they might have been at speed but then, most cars of that time didn't have very good headlamps anyway). The wind noise was characteristic of sports cars before the days of computer-aided design, but it was an unfortunate fact that the MGA generated more cockpit noise with the hood up than with it down.

When it came to the turn of *Autosport* to road test the 1600, John Bolster, as a competitive motorist, saw the new MGA in a different light. Whilst the car was built as a high-speed sports touring car, he saw that many buyers of the car would use it for club racing. So he went off to Silverstone and put it through its paces. Driving to find the car's limits, he concluded that '. . . it would take a clumsy driver indeed to run out of road'. Bolster found it a very controllable car, whatever he did with it, though he did express the view that it would be a little heavy to be used as a competition car in standard road trim.

*The MGA 1600
in production on
the line at
Abingdon.*

But then again, anyone wanting to use the MGA 1600 in regular competition would have wanted to improve the state of tune of the car, using any one of the wide range of performance options available, and reduce the car's weight as well. Funnily enough, the roughness of running at high engine speeds reported by the *Autocar* tester occurred in the car driven by John Bolster, too. He was a man with an enviable record of competitive driving and an acute sense of awareness for an engine's state of tune, which means that, as the two tests were not conducted on the same vehicle, the problem, almost certainly

135

Darlene Hard, the celebrated American tennis player of the 1950s, is seen here with her MGA 1600 before it was shipped to the United States, even though it was a right-hand drive car. Note that the dark section of the side light is at the top, as these were used in the US as amber parking lights. The wing mirror was a typical 'racing-style' accessory of the time.

one of balance, was common to the 1600 engine. John Bolster's report talks of the engine going through a rough period, when both noise and vibration become somewhat pronounced, as the maximum speed of the car is approached, putting the problem above 5,000rpm. The only thing that can be reasonably concluded here is that while different engines performed differently, all would produce the problem at something over 5,000rpm.

The gearbox on the *Autosport* test car, on the other hand, seems not to have given Mr Bolster any problem, as he was full of praise for its handling under all conditions, describing it as '. . . a splendid component; it would be hard to better the easy and precise operation of that short and rigid lever'. He went on to say that the clutch was well able to cope with the bigger engine and that the brakes were entirely free from vice and could not be made to fade. That last comment was almost certainly a relative statement, as MGA brakes (even disc ones) *can* be made to fade, but it probably took much longer with the MGA 1600 than with many other cars.

It seems John Bolster tried quite hard to lever 100mph out of his test car, but didn't quite make it, 97.1mph (156.3km/h) being his best, though he was convinced that with a good smooth surface and decent weather conditions, it would be possible. He also observed that the hood would create a fair amount of wind resistance, judging from the noise when it was erected (and he drove his test with the hood up for most of the time, it seems), and suggested that was another factor in his failure to make the 'ton'. On fuel consumption, the *Autosport* car seems to have done better than most, having turned in a genuine 26mpg (10.9l/100km), even after driving hard. Mr Bolster was clearly pleased with his test drive and impressed with the car.

EXTRACTING MORE FROM THE MGA 1600

We have already looked briefly at the HRG-Derrington aluminium alloy cylinder head conversion and at two alternatives for supercharging the 1600 engine. We've also listed the factory-approved conversion kits, covering Stages Two to Five levels of tuning. It's time now to take a closer look at how it was possible (and still is, if you can find the parts) to extract a little more power, safely, from the 1,588cc 'B' Series BMC engine. It was always possible, of course, to follow the cheap route of planing thirty or forty thousandths of an inch from the cylinder head to increase the compression ratio, but the risk of causing the valves to come into contact with the pistons must be a very good reason for recommending serious caution in pursuing this route.

One factory-approved accessory kit which was a valuable addition, even if no performance-enhancing work was to be done on the engine, was the oil cooler kit. Anybody who has ever driven a 'B' Series engine hard over a long distance will know that a drop in oil pressure, resulting from an increase in oil temperature, is not uncommon. The oil cooler kit was a very sound investment, considering the potential cost of bearing replacement and major engine surgery which could result from the failure of the lubrication system arising from overheating. Having fitted the oil cooler kit, the MGA owner could then progress to selecting the right route for improving the performance of the engine, to suit both car and pocket.

Supercharging was without doubt the physically easiest way of achieving a power improvement on the 1600 engine (or any other, for that matter), not least because it did not involve interfering with the internals of the engine. Post-war superchargers were much less complicated than those previously fitted to MGs, in that they were no longer bolted on to the front of the engine, directly dog-driven from the crankshaft, and they no longer had the complicated induction systems of pre-war supercharged engines. The PECO or Judson superchargers were both fairly simply bolted on and were belt-driven. There was no longer a long induction pipe running from the front-mounted blower to the cylinder head, the carburettor being mounted directly on to the body of the supercharger which was attached directly to the inlet manifold, so shortening the distance that the fuel/air mixture had to travel.

One distinct advantage of this supercharger kit was that there were no tell-tale signs of its existence on the car once installed, except perhaps for a slightest whine which is characteristic of a supercharger's presence. The ripe, but not unpleasant, exhaust note further subdued the whine, so the innocent bystander would not know that anything had been done to change the performance of the car – only the driver or passenger would be aware from the shunt in the back under acceleration.

The value package included the supercharger itself, a Roots type with a casing manufactured for PECO by Sir George Godfrey & Partners, manufacturers of precision engineered components for the aviation industry, as well as the drive belt (and a spare), a PECO extractor exhaust system (complete with the then popular PECO exhaust booster at the end of the tailpipe), the dual-belt pulley and all the nuts and bolts for the installation. The instructions provided the guidance for fitting the kit and the results were really quite startling.

On the road, the value of the supercharger was demonstrated by a 0–60mph time of 11.2 seconds, compared with the 14.2 seconds of the production 1600; 0–90mph took only 36.4 seconds which, for a 1600cc car, was a pretty creditable performance. Furthermore, the supercharger turned the MGA 1600 into a genuine 100mph-plus sports car, alongside the other 1600 MGA variant, the Twin-Cam. Maximum speeds in the gears were 30mph (48km/h) in first, 50mph (80km/h) in second, 73mph (118km/h) in third and 104mph (167km/h) in top. That compares very favourably with the Twin-Cam's maxima of approximately 31, 50, 81 and 113mph (50, 80, 130 and 182km/h). Pretty fair, considering the price differential of over a couple of hundred pounds. What was more, the touring fuel consumption comparison of the Twin-Cam was 27.6mpg (10.3l/100km), while the PECO-supercharged 1600 was close to 31mpg (9.1l/100km)!

As has already been said, in the United States and Canada, the MGA 1600 owner could achieve much the same level of performance by buying the Judson supercharger. The installation of this kit was very similar to the PECO system, though it retained the original exhaust system. Performance in power, road speeds and fuel consumption was comparable, too. It was also belt-driven, with an eccentric adjuster on the supercharger pulley spindle to take up belt slack. However, the Judson seemed to suffer from greater induction roar than its

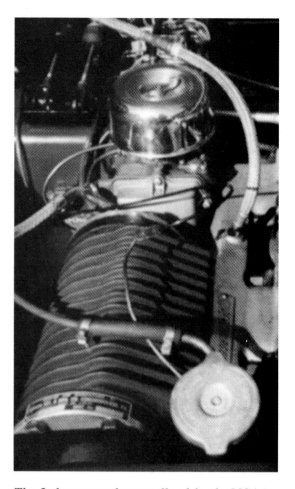

The Judson supercharger offered for the MGA in the United States.

British counterpart and so an air cleaner/silencer was introduced for installation on to the carburettor to bring the noise down to a more acceptable level. Both PECO and Judson blowers were quite popular among the road-going MGA fraternity, but were not suitable for the out-and-out competition driver for, apart from anything else, superchargers were not favoured by racing regulations or competition organizers.

PUTTING MORE IN TO GET MORE OUT

The HRG-Derrington alloy cylinder head conversion to the 1600 was the racing driver's alternative to factory-approved tuning kits, not least because, by comparison, it gave quite startling results for the buyer's money. This conversion did involve tampering with the internals of the engine, in that it was a direct replacement for the original cylinder head of the 'B' Series BMC-manufactured MGA engine. It has already been suggested that it could well have been a factory original equipment specification, had logic prevailed, but the economics of volume production dictated what left Longbridge for Abingdon and other plants, not the desirability of a particular limited-production variation from standard.

The Derrington head came already assembled, with inlet and exhaust guides, valves and springs fitted and valves ground in. The comprehensive installation instructions, together with all the nuts, bolts and washers needed to remove the original head and install the alloy one. Standard carburation with the HRG head was 1¾in SUs, though Derrington pointed out that optimum results would be obtained with Weber 40 or 42 DCOE twin-chokes. A new induction pipe was part of the kit anyway, so the customer had to make the decision between SU and Weber carburettors at the time of purchase, though they could then simply bolt on the selected carbs and manifold once the head was fitted. The only thing which needed replacement in this installation was the water valve for the heater, which had to be repositioned, if the car was fitted with a heater, though an adaptor was available for less than a pound (just under two dollars).

The principle of the HRG-Derrington head was that, being aluminium alloy, it would run cooler than the original iron head of the 'B' Series engine. The separate inlet ports on the alloy head were also a significant benefit, as the inflow of fuel/air mixture was greatly improved and with the cooler running, less mixture was required (lean burn engines long before that phrase was coined?). In tests it had been established that, even with standard carburation and exhaust manifold, the alloy head had produced a 25 per cent improvement in power, a 10 per cent improvement in fuel consumption and a reduction in running temperature of almost 20 degrees C, so keeping the oil temperature down and helping prolong bearing life. If the owner had wanted to go to the limit, high compression bowl-in-piston combustion chamber pistons could be fitted, giving 9:1 ratio, together with a pair of 42DCOE Webers to realize over 108bhp with minimal effect on fuel consumption, just beating the standard power output of the Twin-Cam.

MGA 1600 GOES DE LUXE

In April 1960 Abingdon announced its intention to withdraw the Twin-Cam from the MGA line-up, as the pushrod 1600 had now established itself in the market and, in its first year, sold getting on for 20,000 cars, mostly to North America, pulling back its market share from the decline of the 1500 and making some ground in the process. The last Twin-Cam was built in June and a new variant of 1600 was offered – no doubt to use up as many parts left in the Twin-Cam bins as possible – which was labelled the 1600 De Luxe. The most obvious changes made to the new model were the road wheels, which probably looked familiar, as they were the centre-lock disc type from the Twin-Cam, accompanied by disc brakes all round, as on the Twin-Cam.

The seats from the Twin-Cam, together with the interior trim, were transferred over to the De Luxe MGA 1600, so that it was effectively a Twin-Cam with a pushrod

---
MGA 1600 Mark I De Luxe

VEHICLE CONSTRUCTION
Rectangular-section steel-tube chassis with
fabricated scuttle 'bridge' and pressed steel body
structure with pressed steel panels

ENGINE

Crankcase/cylinder block	One piece cast iron
Cylinder head	Cast iron ohv
Cylinders	4
Compression ratio	8.3:1 standard (others optional)
Cooling system	Pressurized, thermo-syphon and pump
Bore and stroke	75.39 x 89mm
Engine capacity	1,588cc
Main bearings	Three shell-type
Valves	Single camshaft ohv pushrod/rocker
Fuel supply method and type	SU high pressure electric pump
Quoted max. power	79.5bhp @ 5,600rpm
Quoted max. torque	87lb/ft @ 3,800rpm

BRAKES

Type	Dunlop disc brakes front and rear with mechanical handbrake linkage
Size	11in

TRANSMISSION

Clutch type	Single dry plate Borg & Beck A6G
Gearbox ratios	R, 20.468:1; 1, 15.652:1; 2, 9.520:1; 3, 5.908:1; 4, 4.300:1; standard
Final drive ratio	Hypoid bevel 4.300:1 standard

SUSPENSION AND STEERING

Front suspension	Independent coil/piston dampers
Rear suspension	Semi-elliptic/piston dampers
Steering type	Rack and pinion, 2.66 turns
Wheel type and size	Vented disc 4J x 15in centre-lock
Tyre size and rating	5.90 x 15in Dunlop Road-speed

VEHICLE DIMENSIONS (in/mm)

Overall length	156/3,962
Overall width	58/1,473
Wheelbase	94/2,388
Track	
front	47.91/1,216
rear	48.875/1,241

engine. Fitted up with any one of the higher performance kits available, it had much of the potential of the Twin-Cam with none of the average driver's claimed reliability problems – and for something less than the price of the Twin-Cam at that, and running a slightly better fuel consumption, too. In fact, it has been suggested that you should think of the 1600 De Luxe as simply a Twin-Cam car with a pushrod engine.

The production life of the original 1600 was brought to its end in March 1961, after a run of just under two years, bearing in mind the fact that, while it was not announced until mid-summer 1959, the first cars were built in May. The 1600 had enjoyed the distinction of being the model in production when MG celebrated the 50,000th MGA leaving the Abingdon line and by the time it was succeeded by the Mark II 1600, over 31,500 examples of this variant had been built. So it was a success, as was well demonstrated by its competition swansong at Sebring in 1961.

Two MGA 1600 Coupés were entered by Abingdon for the 1961 Sebring 12 Hours

Sebring tempted Abingdon again in 1961 and these two 1600s finished first and second in their class at the hands of Parkinson/Flaherty and Riley/Whitmore.

Race. Sebring was one of the most gruelling sports car races, run in Florida's 85°F (29°C) winter heat on an airfield circuit designed to test cars to their limits. The two MGs, one driven by Californians Jim Parkinson and Jack Flaherty, the other by Brits Peter Riley and John Whitmore, finished first and second in the 1600cc Grand Touring Class, covering 175 and 173 laps respectively in the twelve hours. MGAs were no strangers to Sebring, of course, having run in the 12 Hours in 1956, 1957, 1959 and 1960. It was a tremendous achievement and the perfect platform from which to launch the MGA 1600 Mark II. . .

10 The 1600 Abroad and the 1600 Mark II

Of course, the MGA 1600 simply had to be a success overseas and nowhere more so than in the United States. For if it failed in that market, then it would have failed almost totally, having been developed to tackle the growing competition from other European sports cars on sale there. Like other British sports cars, this vehicle was an important export and combined with them to form a major flagship of Britain's dollar-earning fleet. Indeed in the mid-1950s, cars were close to being Great Britain's biggest dollar earner, second only to the aviation industry.

FIRST IMPRESSIONS OF THE 1600

Given that American sporting motoring has a somewhat different perspective and character from Britain and Europe, it is true to say that it has changed over the years as a direct consequence of the influence on serving men and women during and just after the Second World War. During the war years, most American military, political and press personnel were based in Britain and, despite the standing joke about two great peoples separated by a common language, that common language had a substantial part to play in the development of attitudes towards motoring in Europe.

These people were exposed to British cars of all kinds and found themselves fascinated and a little puzzled at the size and performance of these diminutive machines. Those vaguely interested in or tempted by sports cars were somewhat in awe of their performance, given that many an 1100cc British sports car could at least keep pace with much of what they were familiar with on home ground. It is this awe and fascination which tempted many to take home examples of pre-war British sports cars, from Aston Martin to Triumph alphabetically. Such people made up the staffs of the new generation of post-war American motoring magazines, such as *Road and Track* and *Car and Driver* to name but two of the most enduring.

It was *Road and Track* which first came to the notice of the author, while serving with a joint Anglo-American military team, and it made an immediate impression, as very little of its page space was given over to American cars. What was more, it had a monthly feature entitled 'Salon', in which it had then just recently (May 1959) reviewed the merits and performance of the MG K3 'Magnette', describing that car as: '...for our money, the best MG they ever made'. It may have been, but that is not an issue for these pages: what is of interest here is the way the October 1959 issue of that magazine viewed the new MGA 1600 Roadster.

Of course, it was to be expected that our trans-Atlantic neighbours should take the view that Abingdon had dragged its feet in developing the new MGA model, but the American motor industry was not then suffering from the painful cash-flow and investment shortfalls that plagued British industry at the time. After all, Britain had a crippling national debt to repay and most of its industrial management of the day was

This 1600 chassis, built for display, shows, on the bottom right, its disc brakes for all to see.

either blinkered by that condition or restrained by those who were so blinkered, with the result that investment to improve performance was often overlooked.

Slow in coming or not, *R & T* did take the view that it had been worth the wait. They did point out that the typical American attitude might be one of wonder that such a small increase in engine capacity could do anything useful to improve the performance of the car. However, the road tester then set

about doing his job diligently, by pointing out that the 1600 certainly *did* perform better than its predecessor, the pushrod 1500, though the example they had in their possession at that time was a little too new to take liberties with.

Despite not being able to take the car to its absolute limits, *R & T* was able to secure a realistic impression of the car's potential, deducing that the 16-plus per cent increase in torque and the 10-plus per cent power

MG-A 1600

SPECIFICATIONS

List price	$2485
Curb weight, lb	2050
Test weight	2350
distribution, %	52/48
Dimensions, length	156
width	58
height	50
Wheelbase	94.0
Tread, f and r	47.9/48.9
Tire size	5.60–15
Brake lining area	n.a.
Steering, turns	2.7
turning circle, ft	32
Engine type	4 cly, ohv
Bore & stroke	2.97 x 3.5
Displacement, cu in	96.9
cc	1588
Compression ratio	8.30
Bhp @ rpm	79.5 @ 5600
equivalent mph	96.6
Torque, lb-ft (est).	90 @ 3500
equivalent mph	60.4

GEAR RATIOS

O/d (n.a.), overall	
4th (1.00)	4.30
3rd (1.37)	5.91
2nd (2.21)	9.52
1st (3.64)	15.7

CALCULATED DATA

Lb/hp (test wt)	29.6
Cu ft/ton mile	83.0
Mph/1000 rpm (4th)	17.2
engine revs/mile	3480
Piston travel, ft/mile	2030
Rpm @ 2500 ft/min	4285
equivalent mph	73.8
R&T wear index	70.7

PERFORMANCE

Top speed (4th), mph	103
best timed run	n.a.
3rd (5900)	74
2nd (5900)	46
1st (5900)	28

FUEL CONSUMPTION

Normal range, mpg	25/31

ACCELERATION

0–30mph, sec.	4.2
0–40	6.4
0–50	9.8
0–60	13.3
0–70	19.0
0–80	26.5
0–90	
0–100	
Standing ¼ mile	19.8
speed at end	70

TAPLEY DATA

4th, lb/ton @ mph	190 @ 50
3rd	280 @ 42
2nd	430 @ 32
1st	540 @ 20
Total drag at 60 mph, lb	105

SPEEDOMETER ERROR

30 mph	actual, 30.3
40 mph	39.1
50 mph	43.3
60 mph	47.1
70 mph	66.5
80 mph	76.3
90 mph	86.0
100 mph	

The usual comprehensive road test data was compiled by Road & Track. *They spoke well of the 1600's performance, but weren't too happy about some minor details of trim and design.*

increase were indicative of a larger capacity increase than was to be expected from the additional 99cc of the MGA 1600. The best expression that *Road and Track* could put to the performance increase from this first road test was the gains achieved in pulling power, with 5.6 per cent in top gear, 7.7 per cent in third, 8.8 per cent in second and 8.0 per cent in first. That foretold of a car with the potential to recoup a significant chunk of lost sales.

Out on the road, *R & T* concluded that they now had a true 100mph sports car, just, and that its road manners were very much improved by the provision of disc brakes to the front of the car. The revised sidescreens, with their sliding perspex windows, were praised as a significant improvement on the originals, though the car's poor ventilation came in for some fairly sharp criticism. Recognizing that '*Road and Track*' was based in California, and that a growing number of MGAs would find their way to that part of the United States, this was a perfectly valid criticism.

Handling of the 1600 was reckoned to be much improved over the 1500, simply by virtue of the front disc brakes. This one improvement, combined with the power increase (which was really quite modest), allowed the average driver to take the car closer to the limits of its performance envelope in safety. Remembering the MG house motto 'Safety Fast', it was a very important factor to be able to drive the car faster and harder in safety, for this was one of the key selling features in the American distributor's promotional programme for the MGA.

Road and Track was an unusually discerning magazine as American motoring journals went in those days, being concerned with cars for, as its title implied, road *and* track. The magazine's comments on the MGA 1600 as a potential racing machine therefore make interesting reading. The first conclusion was that the car was too heavy for out-and-out racing, it really being a high performance road car first and foremost. None the less, the club competition potential was recognized and *R & T* described the 1600 as 'the best all-round sports car for use in America, especially for the new enthusiast'.

For all the praise that was given to this new variant of the MGA, *R & T* was still, justifiably, critical of some aspects of the 1600. They felt that Abingdon had not done enough to improve many convenience factors of the car in the process of introducing this new version. But again, this was really down to the company having insufficient cash available to modify tooling or invoke any more than the most minor of changes – and from a production point of view, the changes which were made were quite minor. *R & T* felt that the pedals were too close to each other, which is a valid point for a driver with wide feet: the seats were thought not to be of sufficiently 'bucket' shape, so not retaining their occupants securely enough (a point with which the author has to agree). The luggage compartment came in for its usual share of criticism, though the additional point about having to fumble for the internal lock release with hands full was also made.

Then there was the battery compartment. The writer was quite scathing about this, saying that to gain access to the battery, you must first remove the tonneau cover, then raise the side-curtain storage case (bag), then put up the top (!). After this, they say, you're getting close. Now all you have to do is remove the sheet metal screws (self-tappers) and the rear floor comes out, exposing the battery – if it's still there after being ignored for six months. Certainly, having to do all this just to check the electrolyte levels on a weekly basis could reasonably be seen as a chore. It is reasonable to say that if Abingdon had given this one item really serious thought, it would not have been beyond the wit of a quite junior designer to relocate the battery under the bonnet somewhere.

Road and Track did make the point,

though, that some of the foibles of the MGA were curable by other means. For example, you could buy an external spare wheel carrier to mount on top of the boot-lid and place your luggage inside the boot, provided it was in soft bags – suitcases and MGAs never did go together and designer luggage was not yet in general fashion. Alternatively, you could have bought a luggage carrier and put your suitcases on the outside, in the fashion of the early grid-mounted trunks. It would be interesting, in fact, to read a *Road and Track* 'Salon' review of the MGA now, thirty years after its introduction and see if the reverence held for the K3 (twenty-five years after that car was built) would be matched for the 'A'.

OTHER AMERICANS EXAMINE THE 1600

Another American magazine which had a strong leaning towards European sports cars was *Sports Cars Illustrated (SCI)*. They published an MGA 1600 road test report in their September issue of 1959 (which would have appeared at almost the same time as *Road and Track*, since *R & T* was always published a month ahead of the masthead date, whereas *SCI* appeared during the month of publication). This magazine was slightly more general in its field of interest, covering American and European sporting motoring, including such eccentric activities as 'Stock' car (meaning production car) and single-seater racing round oval tracks, such as Daytona and the mighty Indianapolis, as well as road cars.

Like *R & T*, *SCI* were strong in their criticism of the boot-lid release mechanism, making the very logical point that, apart from there not being enough space in the luggage compartment, it would have been inexpensive and very sensible to have had an external lock on the boot-lid, partly from the point of view of security and certainly from

the point of view of ease of access – again making the point that the owner might have an armful of packages to put into the boot and so find it very awkward to locate the ring pull release inside the car. Seating space was considered adequate, though no comment was made about the occupants sliding about on the standard seats, which certainly seemed more appropriate to a small van than a sports car.

In a road test which covered over 2,000 miles (3,200km), the *SCI* testers took their test MGA 1600 from the US distributor, Hambro Automotive Corporation, in New York, out through that state into New Jersey, Pennsylvania, Ohio, Indiana and Illinois. Upon handover, the car had covered just over 800 miles (1,300km), so was considered run-in, but in need of more 'bedding-in' before being driven too hard. So the first part of the road test in the 1600 covered the length of the Jersey Turnpike, driving out into Pennsylvania, where the speed limit was already a 'silly' 65mph (105km/h), though the car at least had a chance to put a few more miles on the clock without stress.

On the second day of the test programme, which started early in the morning, the MGA was driven out on to the open road, with the pedal pressure on the throttle being around what the testers had previously used to

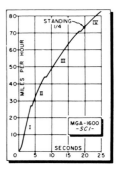

This is the performance graph produced by Sports Cars Illustrated, *based on their road test.*

achieve 60–65mph (95–105km/h). On checking the speedometer, as they passed another
British sports car, un-named, but of 2-litre
engine capacity (so it didn't take too much
mental agility to deduce which one!), the
testers realized they were doing 75mph
(120km/h). As they progressed, now with
almost 1,300 miles (2,100km) on the clock,
the running temperature had dropped from
365°F (185°C) to 347°F (175°C), with a
resultant rise in oil pressure of just over
5lb/in² (0.35kg/cm²). Now, they were able to
put the pressure on!

After some country driving, during which
the general roadholding and handling of the
1600 were put to the test and closely compared with its predecessor, the MGA 1500,
the car was driven on the toll road north to
Chicago, during which time the testers
observed that half-throttle was more than
adequate to bring down the wrath of the local
gendarmerie upon them! As a consequence,
it was realized that the throttle pedal could
have been better placed for comfortable driving at lower speed pedal settings, whereas it
was at its best near to flat out. It was the
braking performance which really showed
itself on the country roads, though.

Once more, road testers had found that the
addition of front disc brakes had transformed
the MGA into something much more than the
addition of 99cc engine displacement might
suggest. The realization for the average
sports car driver that this car could really be
driven in safety, fast, was immediate in the
MGA 1600, whether the driver had previously driven an MGA 1500 or another make
of car equipped with drum brakes. The *SCI*
testers had an excellent opportunity to put
their car's Lockheeds to the ultimate test as
they drove down the Indiana toll road at
dusk. As they cruised happily along the road,
with not a care in the world, suddenly a very
large 'care' projected itself into their path at
a distance of about thirty feet. It was a large
mule deer, which leapt out from the wide

central median right into the headlamp
beams of the MGA. Luckily, the road was dry
and the driver slammed on the brakes, veer-
ing the car to his left at the same time to try
to avoid putting a very large piece of minced
venison in the passenger compartment!
Fortunately, the Lockheed discs did not let
them down and the car and test team
returned to New York unscathed.

Other American magazines which put the
1600 through its paces included *Auto Age*,
Car and Driver, *Sports Car Graphic*, *Speed
Age* and *Motor Trend*. All drew very similar
conclusions to those of *Road and Track* and
Sports Cars Illustrated. Most were unhappy
about the throttle setting for American cruising speeds, the difficulty of access to the boot
and the lack of space within it. A couple commented, like *R & T*, about the design of the
seats and the poor interior ventilation, both
valid criticisms about which Abingdon could
almost certainly have done something.

THE 1600 ELSEWHERE IN THE WORLD

There weren't many MGAs exported anywhere outside North America, though
Australasia was a passable market that
seemed to have quite a few patient hopefuls
who would place a deposit and wait over a
year for their new MG. Though sales of the
1500 MGA had been very limited, the
Australian press had first published a road
test conducted by Gordon Wilkins in Britain
as an appetizer, but then (*Modern Motor*
and *Sports Car World* among them) had put
the original model through its paces for
themselves. Suitably impressed, while the
Twin-Cam barely touched Australian shores,
they then waited with bated breath for the
arrival of the MGA 1600, about which *Sports
Car World* (*SCW*) was among the first to
report a test.

It was also in September 1959 that *SCW*

road test appeared, under the headline: 'Stand Back for the MGA 1600'. Like the American test cars, this one was not fully run in by the time it reached its press destination, which must have been a little irritating, as it would limit what could be done responsibly with the car over a relatively short test period. However, the test was not representative of the car in Australia, as it was conducted by Gordon Wilkins in France, on the same press release trip organized by BMC as was attended by the correspondents of *Motor Sport* and *Autosport*.

Wilkins followed a route from Lyon to Grenoble, via the Col des Leques, Castellane, the Col des Luens and Cannes to Antibes. During his drive, he too was to find the Lockheed disc brakes a tremendous bonus to the handling of the car though, like the American *Sports Cars Illustrated* testers, he found the throttle pedal inconvenient at middle speeds. In fact, Wilkins was the first to describe specifically why the pedal was awkward – it was simply positioned too high for the heel to rest on the floor at much less than full throttle. This tester also observed that, because of the throttle position, it was very difficult to 'heel-and-toe' the throttle and brake pedals for rapid down changes of gear.

Gordon Wilkins said nothing about the ventilation of the MGA, but that is probably more to do with what was familiar to him than what was thought to be an important ingredient of a car to be driven in Antipodean climes. Imagine, if you will, a drive from Adelaide to Melbourne with the standard ventilation of an MGA. Or even a drive up the East Coast road from Sydney to Brisbane, or then again, just pottering about anywhere locally in Australia. Then you would have concern for the car's ventilation – and the fan fitted to the optional heater wouldn't have been a great deal of help, as it was a bit puny for operation in tropical regions.

Like most other road testers, Wilkins came up with a few other criticisms, among them the positioning of the starter button, which was a pull type switch positioned awkwardly just behind the steering wheel rim. Then there was the point about the distance between the driver's chest and the steering wheel with the seat set for a short driver. Here, the tester made the valid point that the steering wheel was too close to the driver for the development of a polished driving style, the optional telescopic adjustment moving the wheel out from the dash, not away from the driver.

By April 1960 a couple of MGA 1600s had finally found their way to Australia and *Sports Car World*, with the help of the Sydney dealer, found an owner willing to part with his new-found treasure for long enough to allow one of their correspondents, Doug Blain, to put the car through its paces 'on site', rather than leaving readers with a European impression of the car. Funnily enough, the owner of this car was a man named Gordon Wilkins (not related to the journalist in any way). Doug Blain's road test revealed nothing new about the MGA 1600, just that it did seem to settle into Australian road conditions very well though he, like others before him, found it difficult to reach that magic three-figure road speed in the test. His closing comments included reference to the car's fantastic handling, equalling many a car of much higher price, that the seats were still 'lousy', steering 'wonderful' gear shift 'snicky'. He liked the car.

Apart from North America and Australia, the latter being a market for local assembly of cars from 'CKD' ('Completely Knocked Down') kits, a very few cars slipped into New Zealand and Southern Africa (another local assembly market). Other left-hand-drive versions found their way into South America and Continental Europe in relatively small numbers. Indeed, partial assembly from 'SKD' (Semi-knocked Down) kits of MGAs were built in some of the least expected areas of the world, such as Brazil, Egypt, Mexico, the Philippines and even Cuba (how many readers remember the double-decker bus deal fronted by Donald Stokes for Leyland in the early 1960s?). Local assembly of cars in overseas markets was encouraged in the 1950s, as it gave importing countries keen to expand their manufacturing bases an opportunity for local labour input to products being sold in their markets. Because of the restrictions on car imports into the Republic of Ireland, this too was a market for kit assembly of the MGA.

In all these locations, too, the 1600 was well received and little comment was made about ventilation, either because it wasn't a problem, or more likely, because something akin to air conditioning was not expected in those market. It may not have been *expected* in North America, of course, but that cars with better ventilation were available there, and often bigger cars for less money, it was a case of drivers having had the experience with which to compare. By March 1961, of course, the final stage in the development of the MGA was to appear in the form of the MGA 1600 Mark II, but the original 1600 can be judged as nothing less than a successful rejuvenation of the original MGA.

ULTIMATE EVOLUTION – THE MGA 1600 MARK II

Almost a year had passed since the demise of the MGA Twin-Cam, leaving the original 1600 version as the only MGA model available, though in four options – the standard 1600 Roadster, the De Luxe 1600 Roadster, the standard 1600 Coupé and the De Luxe 1600 Coupé. By late 1960 Abingdon and the supreme powers at Longbridge knew the car was due for a facelift and by now, in any event, they wanted to standardize the engine to the 1,622cc version of the now rather

mature 'B' Series BMC engine. So was born the MGA 1600 Mark II. Clearly, this new and last variant of the MGA was the stop-gap between the MGA and its successor, the even more prolific MGB, a car not nearly as pretty as the 'A' and which, despite its larger capacity engine, offered much the same performance but possessed little of the character of its forebear. Even so, the MGB, no doubt trading on the reputation and character of the MGA, sold in far greater numbers and was produced in a wider range of variants, the MGBV8 being the nearest thing to an exciting car of all of them.

But back to our story and the last of the MGAs, the 1600 Mark II. Main changes in the new model from the original 1600

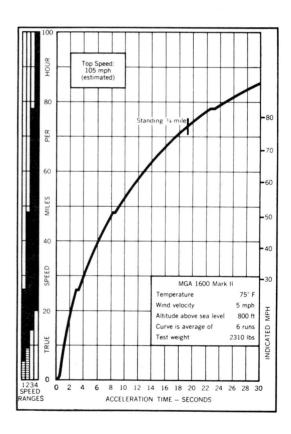

This was Car & Driver's *performance chart for the 1600 Mk II.*

The 1600 Mark II looked very little different at a glance from the Mark I until you did a second take on the radiator grille (right) which, when viewed at an oblique angle, showed itself to be recessed at the bottom of the surround.

Scuttle badging now displayed the '1600 MkII' script.

included the new 16GC type engine of
1,622cc (the bore was now increased to
76.2mm, whilst the stroke remained 89mm),
a long-awaited higher final drive ratio (now
raised to 4.1:1), the introduction of seat belt
mounting points, modified tail lights and a
few other detail changes, including the most
obvious visible change, a revised radiator
grille in which the slats now stood vertical
within the chrome frame, creating a ledge at
the bottom of the grille. While the tail lights
were not particularly attractive on this new
1600, the changed grille was perhaps the
least elegant aspect of the Mark II.

The tail lights were now of a single
unit type, combining stop, tail and
flasher units all in one, mounted horizontally
directly underneath the bottom edge of the
boot lid. They looked what they were, the

*The revised, and horizontal, tail
light of the 1600 Mark II.*

This rear-end view of a 1600 Mark II Coupe shows to good advantage the tail-light cluster in relationship to the rest of the car, the bootlid badging and the luggage rack.

consequence of rooting through the corporate parts bin to find a single lamp unit with amber direction flashers with the stop and tail lights. Trim inside the car was much the same as before, except that the dashboard and inside scuttle were covered with vinyl and a material called 'Novon'. Badging included the placing of the '1600 Mk II' legend behind the shroud air vents and on the boot-lid (below the chromed cast 'MG' badge). The same colour range was offered as on both the previous model and the later Twin-Cam; this included: Black, Ice Blue, Old English White, Alamo Beige, Chariot Red and Dove Grey. Green was, oddly enough, no longer offered as a standard colour on the MGA, so the less than attractive Tyrolite Green was gone. Special colours were provided on cars to individual order.

With a capacity increase of only 34cc between the engines of the 1600 and the Mark II, the performance improvement could hardly be expected to be sparkling, though the higher compression ratio of the 1,622cc unit provided a power output of 90bhp. The 1.5mm-odd increase in valve head diameter of both inlet and exhaust wouldn't have made much contribution to the improved power, though gas flow would have benefitted slightly. Valve timing remained the same as that of the original 1600 (16/56/51/21 degrees) and the installed unit looked just the same as its predecessor, except perhaps for the yellow fan carried over from the later 1600.

With the 4.1:1 final drive ratio, the overall gear ratios with the standard gearbox became 14.924:1, 9.077:1, 5.633:1 and 4.1:1, giving 18.1mph (29.1km/h) per 1,000rpm and a top speed at 5,800rpm (300rpm more than the engine speed for maximum power of 90bhp) of 105mph (170km/h). The pushrod

The dashboard of the Mark II showed only minor trim refinements.

MGA 1600 Mark II

VEHICLE CONSTRUCTION
Rectangular-section steel-tube chassis with fabricated scuttle 'bridge' and pressed steel body structure with pressed steel panels

ENGINE

Crankcase/cylinder block	One piece cast iron
Cylinder head	Cast iron ohv
Cylinders	4
Compression ratio	8.3:1 standard (others optional)
Cooling system	Pressurized, thermo-syphon and pump
Bore and stroke	76.2 x 89mm
Engine capacity	1,622cc
Main bearings	Three shell-type
Valves	Single camshaft ohv pushrod/rocker
Fuel supply method and type	SU high pressure electric pump
Quoted max. power	90bhp @ 5,500rpm
Quoted max. torque	97lb/ft @ 4,000rpm

BRAKES

Type	Lockheed disc brakes front, drum brakes at rear
Size	11in disc front; 10 x 1¾in drum rear

TRANSMISSION

Clutch type	Single dry plate Borg & Beck 8A6G
Gearbox ratios	R, 19.516:1; 1, 14.924:1; 2, 9.077:1; 3, 5.633:1; 4, 4.100:1; standard
Final drive ratio	Hypoid bevel 4.100:1 standard

SUSPENSION AND STEERING

Front suspension	Independent coil/piston dampers
Rear suspension	Semi-elliptic/piston dampers
Steering type	Rack and pinion, 2.66 turns
Wheel type and size	Vented disc 4J x 15in stud mounted
Tyre size and rating	5.60 x 15in Gold Seal

VEHICLE DIMENSIONS (in/mm)

Overall length	156/3,962
Overall width	58/1,473
Wheelbase	94/2,388
Track	
front	47.5/1,206
rear	48.75/1,238
Overall height	50/1,270

MGA was at last a genuine 100mph-plus sports car. The optional close ratio gearbox gave ratios of 10.025:1 in first, 6.642:1 in second, 5.199:1 in third and, of course, 4.1:1 in top. These close ratios, combined with the almost 12 per cent power improvement and the brakes retained from the 1600, made the MGA 1600 Mark II a much more exciting car to drive than the original 1500 and brought its performance envelope a great deal closer to that of the MGA Twin-Cam, while retaining the simplicity of a pushrod engine.

THE 1600 MARK II ON THE ROAD

The two things which seem to have most impressed the road testers about the 1600 Mark II were the marked increase in power output to 90bhp from 79.5bhp (together with a corresponding increase in torque to 97lb/ft from 87lb/ft) and the higher final drive ratio, which together provided a superb inexpensive sports car that was expected to hold the market for the MGA until its successor was available to take its place, answering some of the criticisms of owners and testers for a car with a higher cruising speed at a given

The 1962 Monte Carlo Rally saw the Morley twins win the 2,000cc Class in an MGA 1600 Mark II.

Then Sebring beckoned once more, with an Abingdon entry of three cars, though this time the best the MGAs could do was to finish.

MG-A MKII

DIMENSIONS

Wheelbase, in	94.0
Tread, f and r	47.5/48.8
Over-all length, in	156
width	58
height	50
equivalent vol, cu ft	262
Frontal area, sq ft	16.1
Ground clearance, in	6.0
Steering ratio, o/a	n.a.
turns, lock to lock	2.7
turning circle, ft	31.3
Hip room, front	48
Hip room, rear	n.a.
Pedal to seat back, max	42
Floor to ground	9.0

SPECIFICATIONS

List price	$2485
Curb weight, lb	2050
Test weight	2340
distribution, %	52/48
Tire size	5.60–15
Brake swept area	350
Engine type	4 cly, ohv
Bore & stroke	3.0 x 3.5
Displacement, cc	1624
cu in	99.1
Compression ratio	8.90
Bhp @ rpm	90 @ 5500
equivalent mph	99.5
Torque, lb-ft (est).	100 @ 3500
equivalent mph	63.3

CALCULATED DATA

Lb/hp (test wt)	27.1
Cu ft/ton mile	81.5
Mph/1000 rpm (4th)	18.1
engine revs/mile	3320
Piston travel, ft/mile	1935
Rpm @ 2500 ft/min	4290
equivalent mph	77.5
R&T wear index	64.2

GEAR RATIOS

4th (1.00)	4.10
3rd (1.37)	5.63
2nd (2.21)	9.08
1st (3.64)	14.9

SPEEDOMETER ERROR

30 mph	actual, 28.5
60 mph	57.0

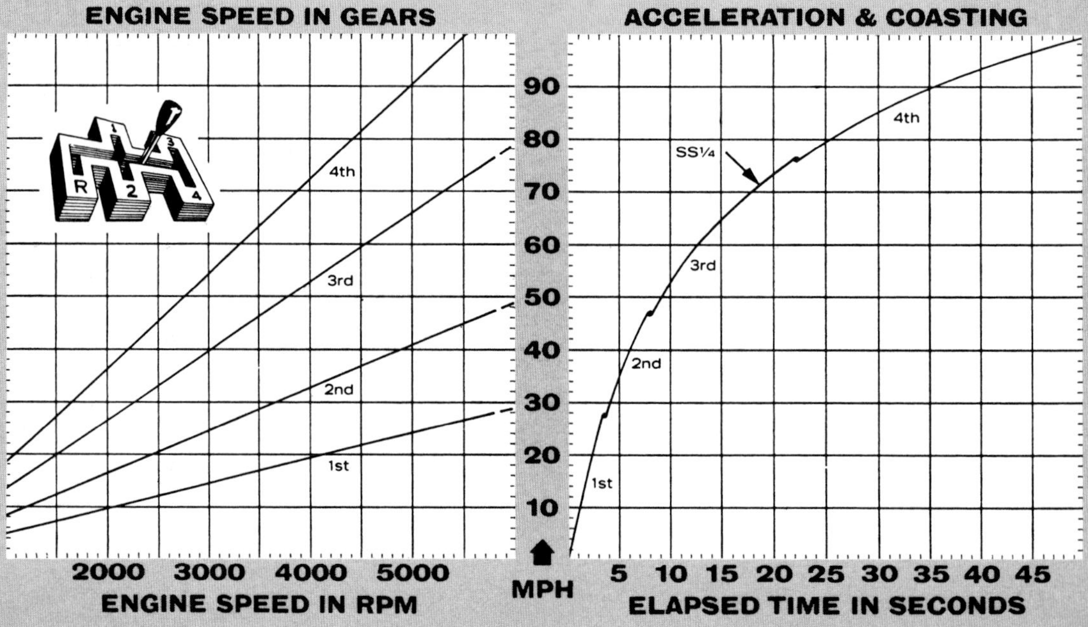

ENGINE SPEED IN GEARS

4th
3rd
2nd
1st

2000 3000 4000 5000
ENGINE SPEED IN RPM

ACCELERATION & COASTING

90
80
70
60
50
40
30
20
10
MPH

4th
SS¼
3rd
2nd
1st

5 10 15 20 25 30 35 40 45
ELAPSED TIME IN SECONDS

PERFORMANCE

Top speed (5800), mph	105
best timed run	n.a.
3rd (6000)	79
2nd (6000)	49
1st (6000)	29

FUEL CONSUMPTION

Normal range, mpg	25/31

ACCELERATION

0–30mph, sec.	4.0
0–40	6.0
0–50	9.3
0–60	12.8
0–70	18.0
0–80	25.4
0–100	
Standing ¼ mile	18.7
speed at end	71

TAPLEY DATA

4th, lb/ton @ mph	200 @ 50
3rd	290 @ 44
2nd	430 @ 35
Total drag at 60 mph, lb	112

Finally, Road & Track *found a true 100mph-plus MGA other than the expensive Twin-Cam. They actually managed to extract 105mph out of the 1,622cc-engined Mark II and were well pleased.*

engine speed. For example, 85mph (137km/h) was now achieved at an engine speed of just under 4,700rpm, instead of nearer to 5,000rpm. The resultant improvement in fuel economy was an additional bonus, as it was now easily possible to achieve over 30mpg (9.4l/100km) at quite respectable cruising speeds.

Back in the United States, the principal market place, *Road and Track* greeted the Mark II with a combination of enthusiasm and despair. Enthusiasm for the improvement in acceleration and maximum speed (0–60 now came in 12.8 seconds and they achieved 105mph (169km/h) on the first attempt). Despair at the unchanged seats and luggage space, as well as the lack of a glove box and the still-poor ventilation. *Car and Driver* came up with similar performance and similar criticisms, while both journals returned fuel consumption figures of between 21 and 32 miles per US gallon (11.2 and 7.4 l/100km), dependent upon traffic conditions and exuberance of driving.

In May 1962 *Sports Car Graphic* was loaned a Mark II by Hollywood Sports Cars with absolutely no mileage recorded on the clock. So, after a careful programme of running-in, they took the car off on a rigorous test run which included race track and unmade road. Handling was everything that had been written by others before, though nobody had recorded unmade-road driving, not even the Australians. Even on these roads, and in driving rain, the MGA was found to handle superbly and *Sports Car Graphic* judged the car to be the perfect basis for modified production sports car racing. Equipped, of course, with the optional 4.55:1 final drive ratio and the close ratio gearbox, the acceleration and track performance were everything *Sports Car Graphic* could have expected and fuel consumption was superb, even with the kind of handling this car was given, at between 23 and 28 miles per US gallon (10.3 and 8.4 l/100km).

However, as *Sports Car Graphic* published its test results, the last MGA 1600 Mark II was leaving the line at Abingdon. The last one built was Chassis Number 109070, though there is a story that a car with Chassis Number 109071, a Coupé with a few odd specification features was the last. This is not actually correct, as 109071 was, in fact, issued with that chassis number prior to being sold, originally having been EX197, a development car that had become Syd

The 100,000th MGA, a 1600 Mark II, rolls off the line in 1962.

Enever's personal hack. Registered as KMO326, it had been built as a roadster and was converted to a coupé, how and when is not quite certain. The fact that it acquired odd non-standard components is explained by it having been in the hands of Syd Enever and used for evaluation of all sorts of new components. Finally, it left Abingdon to go to Syd Enever's son, Roger, who used it both as a club racer and for personal transport. It now had MGB front suspension and brakes, as well as Borrani wire wheels. The engine was a 1,622cc unit of Mark II type and the car had the outward appearance of a Mark II – but it was certainly not the last Mark II car. In any event, the end of the road had come for the MGA, as it was having to compete with Alfa Romeo's Giulia 1600 Spider (with its 112bhp and 112mph (180km/h), not to mention Porsche's 356B 1600 Super.

11 The MGA and its Adversaries

When the MGA was first announced to the market, there were, strange as it may seem, no head-on competitors in the domestic market and really only one of similar engine capacity from continental Europe. The Austin Healey 100 had an engine of almost a litre more capacity: the Triumph TR3 had half a litre advantage over the MG and most other British sports cars were either of much bigger engine size or were smaller. However, the MGA was compared on at least one occasion with the TR3 and there was an inevitable comparison drawn between the MGA 1600 and the Austin Healey 3000 when these two were part of the same press launch in France.

THE CHALLENGER FROM ZUFFENHAUSEN

The MGA's primary continental adversary was a car of totally different design and of a much higher price. The Porsche 356 1500 was available in three forms during 1955 – the Coupé, the Cabriolet and the near-immortal Speedster. All three were, of course, rear-engined with the already firmly established

The Austin Healey 100/4 was, along with the MGA, one of the prettiest sports cars of the 1950s decade but, whilst often compared with the Abingdon car, was never a direct competitor.

159

The Zuffenhausen challenge, the Porsche 356C Cabriolet – a 1,600cc car of higher speed, but much higher price.

and highly respected flat-four which had its origins in the 1,100cc Volkswagen power unit designed by Professor Ferdinand Porsche for the 'People's Car' of the 1930s. Porsche's design studio was also responsible for creating the mighty Auto-Union Grand Prix cars which helped to elevate Germany to racing supremacy in that same decade.

Because of Britain's punitive taxation policy in those days, the price of the Porsche range, which was already quite high, was almost doubled by the combination of import duty and purchase tax, especially as the purchase tax was added to the price of the car plus all its costs and after the addition of the import duty, so the duty, which was already a tax in its own right, was taxed again! In

1955 the Porsche 356A 1500 Cabriolet cost around £2,000 delivered, almost twice the price of the MGA 1500 – and while it was quite a motor car, it wasn't twice the car of the Abingdon machine.

The flat-four Porsche engine came in two forms – the standard unit with pushrod valve actuation and the over-head cam quad-cam type which, of course, was much more powerful, creating a true 100mph-plus vehicle, but at a quite staggering price for a steel-bodied production vehicle, albeit one of quite an impressive specification. The pushrod engine was of 1,488cc displacement, with a bore of 80mm, a stroke of 70mm and a compression ratio of 8.2:1, while the quad-cam boasted an extra 10cc, having a larger bore, at 85mm, and a shorter stroke, of 66mm, to give 1,498cc on a compression ratio of 9:1. On the road, the pushrod unit, at 70bhp, had a comparable performance with the 1500 MGA, top speed being roughly the same, though the Abingdon car was more predictable in its handling. On the other hand, the quad-cam Porsche, the GS Carrera (a car which had made, and acquired, its name in the Carrera Panamericana) turned in a genuine 124mph (199km/h) – more than a match for the Twin-Cam MGA of 1957 in performance, but not on price.

By the time the 1600 MGA had arrived, Porsche had already established their 1600 and in 1959 their 356B 1600S, now with a pushrod engine of 82.5mm x 74mm and equipped with 75bhp (not as much as the MGA 1600 pushrod engine), gave a top road speed of 108mph (174km/h), proving Abingdon's point about a clean aerodynamic line doing far more for speed than brute force. While the MGA was aerodynamically 'clean', the German car was 'cleaner'. The Porsche was certainly an exciting car to drive, but with drum brakes all round (albeit very efficient ones). By and large, the MG really did offer better value all round.

The four-cam 356B 1600GS Carrera GT of 1960 turned in a top speed of nearly 130mph and was quite a handler. Most were coupés though, as were most road Porsches, the open-topped cars being less favoured in their homeland. The Carrera was really a contender for the Twin-Cam's crown, though (and a cabrio was offered), but again the price-tags of the two cars had something to say about their relative values. Of course, the Porsche quad-cam engine was essentially a racing engine, which had proved itself a winner against the most powerful opposition, especially when mounted in the 550RS, 718RSK and 718RS60/61 cars built purely for competition, all being capable of speeds around 150mph (240km/h).

By the time the MGA 1600 Mark II was about to be discontinued, the 356B Carrera had become a 2-litre quad-cam machine with 130bhp out of 1,966cc and a road speed of around 130mph (210km/h). By this time, the 356B 1600GTL Carrera Abarth, bodied by Zagato, had been built and had proved on the track that it had a top speed of 136mph (219km/h). At the same time, the 356C was on the horizon, still a 1600, but now giving 108mph (174km/h) on 115bhp – and drum brakes were still a part of the standard specification.

On the road, the 356 1500 proved itself capable of only just over 91mph (147km/h) (and that was the coupé, a more aerodynamic shape), while its 0–60mph time fell short of the MGA's figure, too, at only 17 seconds. Fuel consumption was quite good, averaging 27–32 miles per gallon (10.5–8.8l/100km), with 28 being averaged over a 785-mile (1,263km) road test. The 1600, on the other hand, came home with a much better performance, the engine producing only 70bhp but converting that through efficient gearing and transmission into a top speed of 101.25mph (163.01km/h), a 0–60mph of 15.3 seconds and a fuel consumption somewhat improved over that of the 1500, at 31mpg (9.1l/100km) over nearly 800 miles (1,300km). So, the only real advantage of the Porsche 356B 1600 over the MGA 1600 Coupé was a couple of very cramped rear seats which gave a new meaning to the term 'occasional'. It took the 1600S or the Carrera to provide a hint of that 'neck-snapping' performance with which Porsches were to become associated.

MILAN'S CONTENDER FOR THE CROWN

As the Alfa Romeo Giulietta hit the streets of Italy in 1954, who could have expected it to metamorphose into one of the most exciting and successful open sports cars ever to leave the Portello works? For out of the Giulietta line came first the Giulietta Sprint Coupé, which certainly gave the world a hint of exciting motoring to come. But then, as if to put down a false trail, the Berlina (Saloon) version of the Giulietta was announced in early 1955. This car had no sporting pretensions, but was a sound and reliable small saloon, based on the earlier 1900. Within a year, the Giulietta Sprint and the Giulietta Spyder had become recognized as two cars which really put Alfa Romeo into contention for the title of maker of the finest small sports cars in Europe.

With the reputation Alfa Romeo brought with it from its great catalogue of racing successes, in both long-distance sports car and Grand Prix events, it was hardly surprising that the engine of this new small car was of aluminium alloy construction and featured five main bearings. The cubic capacity was dictated by other considerations than the International Sporting Code's Class F limit of 1,500cc, so ended up at a rather curious 1,290cc, to place it below a 1,300cc taxation class. Bore was 74mm, while the stroke was 75mm, making an almost square (and almost unburstable) power unit which, even in its original form, delivered 80bhp and over 100mph (160km/h).

By 1956, when the Giulietta Spyder had been in production for a year and when the MGA had settled into production, too, the power output of the 1,290cc Alfa engine was increased to 90bhp at 6,500rpm for the announcement of the Spyder Veloce. With a capacity disadvantage of 199cc and a dry weight only slightly lower than the MGA, this little car was to be compared again and again with the MGA, even when they both

The Alfa Romeo Giulietta Spyder was always held up in the American market as the car for the MGA to beat. With its twin-cam, high-revving alloy engine, that was quite a tall order, despite it giving away 200+cc to the Abingdon car, but the MGA established its place in the market on the basis of styling and price.

graduated to 1,600cc engines, for they shared a certain character that was not common to all small sports cars of the time. In Italian, the word is 'Brio' – there is no English equivalent. But both were pure two-seaters, both were very stylish for their time – the English car being styled at Abingdon, the Italian model styled and built by the world-famous coachbuilder Pininfarina, which accounted for a chunk of its two million Lire price tag.

An American road test, reported in October 1956, conducted a very close comparison of the two cars and gave an excellent indication of just how close they were to each other in many ways, except in absolute top speed and, of course, price. For example, the Alfa Romeo was the faster car, just, at a touch over 100mph (160km/h) in standard form, against the MGA's 97mph (156km/h). The Veloce turned in 112.5mph (181.1km/h) on a 90bhp power unit, but the comparison here was between the lower specification Spyder and the 1500 MGA. Handling of both cars was highly praised and braking, both on drum brakes of course, was considered remarkably efficient when compared with production American cars, and was almost completely fade-free on both cars.

In road-holding and steering response, the Alfa came out on top. On fuel consumption, the Alfa scored better than the MGA, by 5mpg. Internally, the Alfa Romeo was better equipped than the MG, with better sound deadening and carpeting, though similar instrumentation. The one body feature which put the Alfa streets ahead in interior comfort during poor weather was the fact that the doors were fitted with wind-up windows, so abolishing the inconvenience of fitting and removing side screens, to say nothing of the comparable weather tightness. The fit of the Giulietta's hood was also superior to the MGA, but in the United States, the price difference was $900, or almost half as much again as for the MG.

There is no doubt that, until the appear-

ance of the Sunbeam Alpine half way through the production life of the MGA, the Abingdon car had no real British challenger in the same capacity class, though one of a smaller engine size did appear in 1957. As a consequence, the Alfa Romeo Giulietta was to be held up again and again as the nearest thing to the MGA, despite its smaller engine and higher price. The price differential between the two cars was entirely justifiable, the materials and specification of the Alfa Romeo's engine specification being a major factor, combined with the coachbuilt bodywork, produced by one of Italy's leading 'Carrozzeria'. The comparisons drawn were a significant accolade to the work of Abingdon's design and manufacturing teams, producing as they did the least expensive sports car available in the United States at the end of 1956. More than that, this was the best-selling British sports car in that market, too.

THE COVENTRY COMPARISON – THE TRIUMPH TR3

The Irish magazine *Motor Racing* produced a comparison, in its July 1957 issue, between the MGA 1500 pushrod-engined car and the Triumph TR3. In terms of physical size, the TR3 was 5in (127mm) shorter than the MGA, 4in (102mm) lower and 3in (76mm) narrower. It had a turning circle 7 feet (2.1m) greater than that of the MG, at 35 feet (10.7m) versus 28 feet (8.6m). With the same number of steering wheel turns from lock to lock, this made the Triumph slightly less manoeuvrable, especially in tight spots.

Styling of the Coventry-built car was different from that of the MGA, in that it was a more snub-nosed, slab-sided design. However, the more square-ended rear aspect of the Triumph meant it had two advantages over the Abingdon machine: the first being a larger boot (with a wider boot-lid, incidentally), the second being external access to the

The Triumph TR3 was less than £100 more expensive than the MGA at any time (and in fact cost less than the Twin-Cam), and was Britain's first true 100mph mass-produced sports car and the first with disc brakes as standard – but it still couldn't dislodge the Abingdon car from its own special place in any market.

spare wheel, which was withdrawn by removing the panel on which the rear number plate was mounted. This revealed the spare wheel sitting snugly in its own compartment beneath the boot floor, so eliminating the need to remove luggage in the event of it being needed to replace a flat on the road.

Like the MGA, the TR3 was equipped with a hood and sidescreens for weather protection, though the doors, instead of being of high-top design, had deep cutaways aimed at providing plenty of elbow room for the enthusiastic driver. However, this design feature meant that the sidescreens were deeper than those on the MGA and consequently provided a weaker weather seal. But this was something the true enthusiast probably didn't even notice when driving at speed. The cockpit area of the TR3 was, however, smaller than the MGA, with 2in (50mm) less hip room, though the seats were of a better shape to keep the occupants in place.

Driving the Triumph led one to suppose

that it was a heavier car than in fact it was. While it was heavier than the MGA, it demonstrated a better 0–60mph time at 10.8 seconds, and a higher top speed at 105mph (170km/h) – a genuine 'ton-up' sports car. This was achieved at a quite modest engine speed, 5,250rpm, as the car ran at 20mph (32km/h) in top gear at 1,000rpm engine speed. Power output from the 1,991cc Standard Vanguard engine was a genuine 100bhp, which went a long way towards making the TR3 a quite exciting sports car.

Whether the Triumph was a more exciting car than the MGA is a topic that will probably never cease being debated. There are those, including road testers, who believe the MG's handling and road-holding to be better, though its acceleration and maximum road speeds could not match those of the Coventry car, unless you compared the Twin-Cam MGA, since that car came much closer to the performance envelope, though the prices did not compare, as the basic 1500

MGA was only very slightly less expensive and the Twin-Cam was quite a bit more costly than the Triumph.

It is interesting to compare the range of optional extras of these two models, as they are remarkably similar in items and in prices. For example, the perennial wire wheel option was £35 for both cars, while a hard-top for either was also the same price at £75, though the MGA had the advantage of being the only one of the two offered as a genuine coupé. Neither car was fitted with a heater as part of its standard equipment and overdrive was available only on the Triumph, priced at £75 again.

Fuel consumption was another interesting comparison, one which perhaps justified the Triumph's larger, 12½ gallon (57 litre), fuel tank. At low road speeds (and who wanted to drive a sports car at low speeds?), there was little to choose between the two cars, but as speeds increased, so did the gap between their respective requirements for fuel. For example, at a steady 30mph (50km/h), the MGA would return 44mpg (6.4l/100km), while the TR3 came home at 43.5mpg (6.5l/100km). At 40mph (65km/h), the gap widened to 47mpg (6.0l/100km) and 41.5mpg (6.8l/100km) respectively, while at 50mph, it went to 43.2 and 38mpg. At high cruise speeds, we have already established that the MGA would return 28–31mpg (9.1–10.1l/100km), while the Triumph fell short of that by 3 or 4mpg.

While the Triumph was not looked upon as a direct competitor for the MGA because of the difference in engine sizes, it is fair to say that many sports car buyers of the time did give the Coventry car a second look, simply because it was a genuine 100mph car and cost little more than the Abingdon vehicle. But once the MGA 1600 was on the road, the situation began to change and more would-be owners took a second look at the higher insurance premiums on the TR3 and decided that the MGA was now so much closer to it

in performance – and was a significantly better-looking car as well – that their money would go on the car from Abingdon.

THE LITTLE CAR FROM HORNSEY

Alfa Romeo had shown the way to many a sports car maker, in proving that a well designed engine of smaller capacity could do the job of many a car of larger power unit. So it came as no surprise to some when a small firm located then in Hornsey, in East London, engineered a lightweight two-seat coupé with an engine displacement of even less than the Alfa Romeo Giulietta at 1,216cc. The company was, of course, Lotus Engineering Limited (as Lotus was then known) and the car was the Lotus Type 14, better known as the Elite coupé, powered by a Coventry Climax 1,216cc single overhead camshaft engine known as the FWE type. This engine was an adaptation of the 1,100cc FWA, the change in the last character of the model designation coming as the direct result of increasing the bore to 76.2mm.

The Lotus Elite came into being as a result of Colin Chapman's conviction that he could produce a car to run in the under-1,300cc Grand Touring class to compete with the best of them – the best at that time being mainly Alfa Romeo, with the Grand Touring version of the Giulietta, the Sprint Coupé. Lotus was, at this time, still establishing itself as a serious competitor in sports car racing, with such fine cars as the XI in particular, which had performed outstandingly well at Le Mans, and the Seven, which was being offered as a kit car for the home builder to assemble and race. The Elite was also to be offered as a kit car, primarily as a means of putting a serious sports car into the hands of less than affluent owners. It was a tactic which would mark future Lotus success.

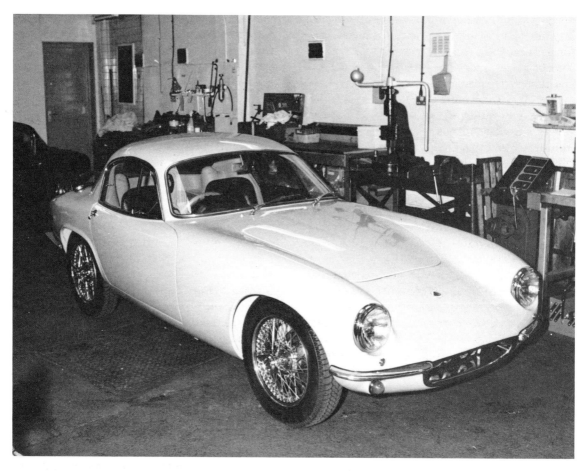

Lotus's Elite broke new ground in the small sports car market in many ways – it was available as a kit car, it had a glass fibre body, it was a coupé and, for a 1,216cc engined car, it was shamefully quick. In kit form, it stood not far away from the MGA on price and was, in fully tuned form, a genuine 110mph+ sports car, but not everybody wanted to put their car together before they could drive it!

Unlike any of its predecessors, the Lotus Type 14, the Elite, was of glass fibre construction, using many aircraft techniques. Light weight was a very important element in the success potential of this little car, though Lotus's design and development team, under John Frayling's supervision and guidance, was also well aware that if this new car was to succeed as a production sports car, it had to be one which people could get into and out of easily. That they were successful is demonstrated by the degree of reverence held today by motoring enthusiasts for the Lotus Elite. In competition, it established an enviable reputation for itself in the hands of such names as Peter Lumsden, Les Leston (who hasn't heard of DAD 10?) and many others too numerous to mention here.

The original body line of the Elite was

designed by an accountant, Peter Kirwan-Taylor, whose work was vetted and checked for aerodynamic efficiency by Frank Costin. The body was the first British production sports car body to be made entirely from fibreglass. The logic of the decision was that fibreglass would withstand much more severe impacts without damage than aluminium, which would dent very easily, and that fibreglass could be moulded to any shape required. Furthermore, where reinforcement was needed, metal plates could be moulded in, sandwiched between layers of glass matting and bonded with the resin bond used to seal the laminates together. The body was actually made up of eight box sections to create the rigidity required and the occupants sat either side of the transmission tunnel.

The suspension system for the car came from the Lotus 12 Formula 2 car, which had proved itself on the track. Overall length was only 12ft (3,658mm), while the car was only 4ft 10in (1,473mm) wide and 3ft 10in (1,168mm) high. The engine was coupled to a BMC 'A' Series gearbox, with modified ratios, and a short propeller shaft took the drive to a hypoid final drive unit. Open drive shafts conveyed drive to the wheels from the rigidly mounted differential, with wire wheels, shod with surprisingly small section tyres (4.90 × 15) completing the mechanical side of the specification. Inside, the car was neat, functional and relatively comfortable. A simple five-instrument dashboard and a wood-rimmed aluminium steering wheel sat before the driver and the floor was carpeted with edge-bound carpets which conveyed an air of quality to the car.

This magic little motor car was a fantastic revelation in the world of sports cars. Race-bred, it proved able to out-corner and out-pace the MGA, which was no reflection on the Abingdon car, as the Lotus was to show a clean pair of Dunlops to both the Alfa Romeo Giulietta Spyder, the Porsche 356 in all but Carrera form and the Alfa Romeo Giulietta Sprint, which was its basic target. Capable of an honest 110mph, the Elite's 0–60mph time was only 11.2 seconds – a pretty respectable time for the 1990s, let alone 1957, the year of its introduction. To make the car even more palatable, it was offered with two SU carburettors as an option, which did nothing for the car's top speed, but helped it along in the intermediate gears. A standing quarter-mile was covered in 18.4 seconds (thirty years later, the Porsche 3.2-litre Speedster made the distance in 15.85 seconds!).

The Lotus Elite was a superb design idea and when you got a good one, it was a fantastic car on the road. However, it was built at a time when Lotus was struggling for cash and so every penny they earned went into building cars for sale, with little attention to spare parts and service. As a result, the company and the car earned a terrible reputation for poor reliability. That was a shame, because if you happened to get a good one, you had a car that was hard to beat on road or track. But if you got a bad one, you were hard pressed to keep it going and to keep the water out and to keep the gel coat on the fibreglass intact and so on. But many an Elite has been rebuilt and the fact that they are commanding prices equal to certain Aston Martins and Ferraris indicates that they clearly had something. Performance on 34mpg (8.3l/100km) might have something to do with it, of course...

COVENTRY'S OTHER CHALLENGER – THE SUNBEAM ALPINE

The Rootes Group, anxious to 'climb on the bandwagon' of popular sports cars, and hungry for export currency, especially dollars, decided to expand on a theme it had begun in 1953. This was a sort of sporting two-seat version of the Sunbeam Talbot 90

THE SPECTACULAR NEW
SUNBEAM *Alpine*

The Sunbeam Alpine came on to the market a little late, but with its wind-up windows and overdrive option, was an attractive touring option to the MGA, though didn't have the same handling.

Saloon, a car which was to be proven by use on rallies. The decision to produce a roadster based on the '90' was as much to do with economics as proven design through rally successes. It was simply cheaper and quicker to adapt the existing model than to start with a 'clean sheet of paper'. Also, since the '90' had been used to win a *Coupé des Alpes* in the 1952 Alpine Rally, it was reckoned that the new roadster, to be called 'Alpine', could do the same. However, the original Alpine was a sales disaster and wasn't a particularly

good performer because of its weight, though today that ruggedness is an attraction to would-be Alpine owners – and it has a certain 'something' in hindsight.

Dropping the original Alpine after only a few dozen cars were sold in the United States and not very many elsewhere in export markets, Sunbeam did not produce another car with sporting pretensions until 1959. Then they produced the new 'Alpine', a sporty little vehicle with lines that had more than a passing resemblance to the original Ford

Thunderbird. The radiator grille, the raised rear fins, everything about the styling of this car seemed to say 'scaled-down Thunderbird'. Taking a leaf out of the Alfa Romeo book, it had wind-up side windows instead of sidescreens. That, of course, added to the weight, but added to the market appeal in North America, too, reckoned Rootes. It was certainly a pretty little car, though the later versions were more attractive, and it sold quite well in the American market at which it was unashamedly aimed.

The Alpine was really more of a sports tourer than an out-and-out sports car, with the result that you didn't see many of them racing, though some were used in rallies. Weather-proofing on the Alpine was very good and from the beginning, it was available with a detachable hard-top – again a bit Thunderbird-ish, though mercifully it did not carry the 'port-hole' of the American car's hard-top. With a live rear axle, leaf rear spring and coil independent front suspension, the car followed custom and practice in the volume sports car market. The three-bearing 1,494cc engine came from the Rapier Saloon, as did the floorpan (though shortened on the way). Wheelbase was 7ft 2in (2,184mm) and the car weighed in at just over 2,140lb (970kg) kerb weight.

The engine produced 78bhp (nett) and was 'over-square' by design, with a bore of 79mm and a stroke of 72mm. Compression ratio was 9.2:1 and maximum power came in at 5,300-rpm (Rootes Group quoted a power output of 83.5bhp at the time, but that was gross power on the bench, without accessories, such as fan and dynamo). A four-speed gearbox was standard, though Laycock overdrive was offered quite soon after the car was announced. Bearing in mind the weight of the car, it had quite a respectable 0–60mph time, at 13.6 seconds, and while it was said to be a 100mph

car, in standard form it really only turned in around 95mph (153km/h).

By 1961 Thomas Harrington, a Sussex coachbuilder whose reputation was based more on building long-distance buses than sporting cars, produced a thoroughly attractive 2 + 2 coupé conversion on the basic Alpine two-seater and, though expensive, it was quite a striking car which, with overdrive on board, made it a true 100mph motor. The original Harrington Alpine Le Mans, as it was named, sold in moderate numbers to North America, but then, when Rootes announced the Mark IV Alpine, they updated the Harrington and that was a truly elegant small Grand Tourer, with well over 100mph available on the right kind of road. They sold all they could build, but sadly didn't build enough, as Harringtons realized that this was not where their future lay.

The Ryton-produced Mark IV Alpine was quite an elegant little car, with the fins reduced to more acceptable proportions and minor line refinements which gave it an elegance that was widely appreciated. The hard-top was revised to fit the newer line, too, giving the car all the creature comforts of a small saloon, combined with something very close to the performance of a sports car – ideal for the man or woman about town. With a quoted speed of 20.2mph (32.5km/h) in overdrive top and a maximum engine speed in top of around 5,500rpm, the car was now endowed with a true potential top speed of over 110mph (175km/h), though its handling and road-holding were no match for the MGA, so journey times aboard the Abingdon car were often much quicker. Priced in between the MGA and the Triumph TR3, the Alpine developed its own market and certainly gave its parents quite a few much-needed dollars, but proved not too much of a threat to the MGA.

Car and Model	Engine type and size	Gearbox	Max. speed mph (km/h)	Fuel consumption mpg (l/100km)	GB price
1955					
MGA 1500	In-line 4 cyl w/cooled 1,489cc	4-speed	96.7 (155.6)	26/29 (10.9/9.8)	£595
Triumph TR3	In-line 4 cyl w/cooled 1,991cc	4-speed	104.7 (168.5)	26/32 (10.9/8.8)	£765
Alfa Romeo Giulietta Spyder	In-line 4 cyl w/c dohc 1,290cc	4-speed	105 (168.9)	30/35 (9.4/8.1)	£1,300
Porsche Super 356 Spyder	Flat-4 air-cooled 1,488cc	4-speed	110.6 (178)	27/30 (10.5/9.4)	£1,320
Morgan Plus Four	In-line 4 cyl w/cooled 1,991cc	4-speed	95.3 (153.3)	27/32 (10.5/8.8)	£795
1958					
MGA Twin-Cam	In-line 4 cyl w/c dohc 1,588cc	4-speed	107 (172.2)	22/28 (12.9/10.1)	£842
Triumph TR3A	In-line 4 cyl w/cooled 1,991cc	4-speed	105 (168.9)	25/31 (11.3/9.1)	£793
Lotus Elite Coupé	In-line 4 cyl w/c sohc 1,216cc	4-speed	112 (180.2)	30/35 (9.4/8.1)	£1,299
Morgan Plus Four	In-line 4 cyl w/cooled 1,991cc	4-speed	95.3 (153.3)	27/32 (10.5/8.8)	£732
Alfa Romeo Giulietta Spyder	In-line 4 cyl w/c dohc 1,290cc	4-speed	105 (168.9)	30/35 (9.4/8.1)	£1,300
Porsche Carrera Speedster	Flat-4 air-cooled dohc 1,498cc	4-speed	125 (201.1)	25/30 (11.3/8.1)	£1,950
1960					
MGA 1600 Mk I	In-line 4 cyl w/cooled 1,588cc	4-speed	100.9 (162.3)	24/31 (11.8/9.1)	£663
Triumph TR3A	In-line 4 cyl w/cooled 1,991cc	4-speed	105 (168.9)	25/31 (11.3/9.1)	£793
Morgan Plus Four	In-line 4 cyl w/cooled 1,991cc	4-speed	95.3 (153.3)	27/32 (10.5/8.8)	£732
Sunbeam Alpine	In-line 4 cyl w/cooled 1,494cc	4 + o/d	99 (159.3)	25/28 (11.3/10.1)	£685
Lotus Elite Coupé	In-line 4 cyl w/c sohc 1,216cc	4-speed	112 (180.2)	30/35 (9.4/8.1)	£1,299
Alfa Romeo Giulietta Spyder	In-line 4 cyl w/c dohc 1,290cc	4-speed	105 (168.9)	30/35 (9.4/8.1)	£1,300
Porsche Spyder 356B 1600S	Flat-4 air-cooled 1,582cc	4-speed	108 (173.8)	29/38 (9.8/7.4)	£1,330
1962					
MGA 1600 Mk II	In-line 4 cyl w/cooled 1,622cc	4-speed	105 (168.9)	25/31 (11.3/9.1)	£663
Morgan Plus Four	In-line 4 cyl w/cooled 1,991cc	4-speed	95.3 (153.3)	27/32 (10.5/8.8)	£815
Elva Courier Sports	In-line 4 cyl w/cooled 1,622cc	4-speed	105 (168.9)	27/33 (10.5/8.5)	£702
Sunbeam Alpine	In-line 4 cyl w/cooled 1,592cc	4 + o/d	101 (162.5)	25/28 (11.3/10.1)	£712
Triumph TR4	In-line 4 cyl w/cooled 1,991cc	4-speed	110 (177)	25/30 (11.3/9.4)	£825
Alfa Romeo Giulia Spyder	In-line 4 cyl w/c dohc 1,570cc	5-speed	109 (175.4)	28/34 (10.1/8.3)	£1,470
Lotus Elite S/E	In-line 4 cyl w/c sohc 1,216cc	4-speed	120 (193.1)	28/35 (10.1/8.1)	£1,495
Porsche Super 75 Cabrio/Coupé	Flat-4 air-cooled 1,582cc	4-speed	115 (185)	28/36 (10.1/7.9)	£1,707

170

12 Enjoying an MGA Today

Enough has already been written in the pages of this book to demonstrate that an MGA – any MGA – is an enjoyable car. Which one you choose to enjoy will obviously depend on your budget. Clearly, the 1500 is generally the least expensive and the Twin-Cam is likely to be the most expensive, both to buy and to maintain. But much of that depends, of course, on the condition of the car you plan to buy, if you don't yet own one.

THE OPTIONS AVAILABLE

The vast majority of would-be MGA owners are probably looking for a fairly simple life, since the likelihood of using one for everyday transport is small. Most enthusiasts are likely to be looking for a car to feed their enthusiasm so, dependent upon their resources, they are likely to be looking for a restoration project or a ready-to-drive example which has, most likely, been restored by a professional. A tatty 1500 or 1600, suitable for that long-term home restoration project, is likely to be bought for quite a modest price, in modern terms, but a fully restored example, probably with a replacement body shell or an extensive selection of new body parts, can cost up to five times as much.

At this distance in time from any car being sold as new, it really doesn't matter whether the car you buy has been raced or rallied, or even thrashed hard on the public roads, because you're almost certainly in for a mechanical rebuild and some measure of chassis/body restoration. Whether you buy a

car to restore, or one which has been restored, the same potential pitfalls have to be looked for, either to rectify or to ensure they have already been rectified. For despite the MGA having been built on a chassis it was, like most sports cars (or any other kind of car of that era), in modern terms, a 'rust-bucket'.

While some cars will have been reasonably well protected from the ravages of time, they almost certainly will have suffered what is delicately referred to as 'first-degree cor-rosion' – that's the kind of rust that will have gone through the paint, but not yet through the structure. Many will have suffered 'third-degree' corrosion in the chassis – where parts of the frame have rusted through and others haven't yet but may do so before long! Just because a car has a chassis doesn't mean it is automatically sound, except for a bit of bodywork. Often, because manufacturers used box-section chassis longitudinals with closed-off ends, giving little or no quick escape for water trapped inside, rusting began from the inside, so by the time the unsuspecting owner found it, it was too late, and the frame was about to break. Luckily, this was not generally a problem with the MGA and even where chassis perforation has occurred, rust normally extends only an inch or so from the edge of the hole and then you reach sound metal again.

Having touched on some of the problems, we'll look a little closer shortly, but first, let's consider what really is available in MGAs today. Clearly, the 1500 and the 1600 are the most readily available – in all conditions

171

This 1600 Roadster, restored (and photographed) by Geoff Barron of the MGA Register of the MG Car Club, is a fine example of what you can do to bring back an MGA to life after years of neglect.

from rough to resplendent at relevant prices. The Twin-Cam and 1600 Mark II are obviously rarer, because there were less of each built in the first place, but if you're determined, then keep looking, for there's bound to be one at a fair price if you're patient. Then it's a question of roadster or coupé? Coupés are also not too common – and if you want a Twin-Cam Coupé, you could be in for a long wait, though 1500 and 1600 versions are around.

CHASSIS AND BODY

One of the worst problems attached to buying an unknown car, be it MGA or any other make and model, is knowing what to look for to decide whether it's worth buying or not. Indeed, knowing whether it's worth buying is a finely balanced decision anyway, for the would-be owner has to decide quite early in his or her search what the budget is to be and in what proportion that budget is to be allocated to purchase and restoration. Common sense suggests that if the purchase is to be on the basis of a restoration project, then the greater proportion of the budget should be allocated to the restoration. The trick is to buy a car and spend less on its restoration than you would expect to spend in total on a restored, but unknown car said to be thoroughly drivable and in pristine condition.

Starting from this, the reader can see just what faces the potential restorer. This one really had suffered from 'metal mites' and would have been abandoned to the scrapman by people with less determination than Geoff Barron.

While the body of the car is the first bit you see of any car, and whilst the MGA *was* built on a chassis, it is the chassis which probably calls for closest scrutiny, for if that major component is badly rusted through, then you have some pretty serious work to contemplate. Many of the cars considered to be restorable today would, twenty-five or thirty years ago, have been scrapped and quickly forgotten. But, today, with the colossal range of spares available from quite reputable sources, many cars that would otherwise have been scrapped have survived. Even so, the would-be MGA owner has to know just what can and cannot be done – and whether it can be done with the car under consideration.

Around the centre section of the chassis longitudinals is the worst area of the chassis frame for serious corrosion. This is the area inboard of the sills, where mud lodges between the inner sill and the chassis, especially on the kerb side of the car, because that's the side which runs in the gutter. The mud dries and sticks like mortar, then it gets wet again, but doesn't fall out, just holds the moisture – and the salt – and slowly deteriorates without the owner being aware of what's happening to the car. Then the chassis is seriously weakened and, because this is a sports car, it finds itself being driven like a sports car, with all the side forces that kind of driving brings, ultimately weakening the

173

MGA PRODUCTION QUANTITIES AND FIRST/LAST CHASSIS NUMBERS

Quantities of all models built, year by year, with first and last chassis numbers by year

MGA Model:	1500 roadster			1500 Coupé			Twin-Cam Roadster			Twin-Cam Coupé			1600 Roadster		
Build Year:	Qty	First C/No:	Last C/No:	Qty	First C/No:	Last C/No:	Qty	First C/No:	Last C/No:	Qty	First C/No:	Last C/No:	Qty	First C/No:	Last C/No:
1955	1043	10101	11144	—											
1956	13394	11145	24608	16	20671	**									
1957	16467	24609	45410	4104	**	**									
1958	14811	45411	61503	1311	**	**	493	501	1029	48	**	**			
1959	6803	61504	—	841	—	—	1256	**	2559	263	**	**	12938	68851	82920
1960	—			—			39	**	2611	12	**	**	15428	82921	99945
1961	—			—			—			—			294	99946	—

MGA Model:	1600 Roadster D/L			1600 Coupé (all)			1600 Mk II Roadster			1600 Mk II Coupé			1600 Mk II Coupé D/L		
Build Year:	Qty	First C/No:	Last C/No:	Qty	First C/No:	Last C/No:	Qty	First C/No:	Last C/No:	Qty	First C/No:	Last C/No:	Qty	First C/No:	Last C/No:
1959	—			1218	**	**	—			—			—		
1960	50	91240	**	1452	**	**	—			—			—		
1961	20	**	**	101	**	**	5137	100352	106025	411	**	**	5	**	**
1962	—			—			2771	106026	109070	95	**	109071	7	**	**

** These cars were built within the chassis number batches quoted for each main model.

Total MGA production, between 1955 and 1962, was 101,082, of which 52,478 were 1500 Roadsters, 6,272 were 1500 Coupés, 1,788 were Twin-Cam Roadsters, 323 were Twin-Cam Coupés, 28,730 were 1600 Mk I Roadsters, 2,771 were 1600 Mk I Coupés, 8,198 were 1600 Mk II Roadsters and 522 were 1600 Mk II Coupés.

frame to the point of fracture – and the driver may still not be aware of the damage. So watch out and check your would-be purchase very carefully.

Floorboards in the MGA were of wood and these could cause their own kind of problem. As the moisture gets to both surfaces of the floorboard, it passes out to the floorboard supporting crossmembers, which also deteriorate, flex and break, so causing another chassis problem to look for. The front end of the frame, around the engine compartment, however, is usually pretty sound, not least because the BMC 'B' Series engine was not renowned for its oil tightness, so helping to spread a coating of protective mixture over

the surface of the frame. However, that area of the frame needs to be checked for the possibility of accident damage, especially if there are signs of liberal applications of body filler in the adjacent body panels.

The worst problem in the front end of the MGA is in the area of the wings. Water thrown up from the road combines with mud and salt, while from above, water drips on and ultimately penetrates the joints of mating surfaces. Finally, the structure gives way under the onslaught and the water mixture penetrates first the paint, then the metal breaks down and we have lace curtain wheel arches instead of solid metal. A similar problem crops up at the back end of the car, where

Replacing the body sills and lower section of the rear wheel arch demands skills that many private owners do not possess, but it doesn't make the restoration project impossible.

The inner scuttle wall is almost like lace curtain in this view.

the rear wing splash plates and aprons suffer from the constant bombardment of salt-water mixed with mud, causing their eventual perforation and allowing the lethal mix then to get to the inner surfaces of the wings themselves with expensive consequences.

Other areas include the rear shroud where the roof of a coupé joins the body. The rust can be so bad that the roof has actually parted company from the body at the rear quarters, so that the windscreen pillars are all that hold the car together. That's not too common an occurrence, but it has been found on MGAs, so again, check your prospective new purchase very carefully before you are parted from your hard-earned cash. Check also door structures, for although aluminium

panels don't deteriorate as quickly as steel, the structure is steel and does rust. The aluminium bonnet also has a steel frame, though oil film usually protects the structure, so preserving the whole intact.

THE ENGINE AND GEARBOX

While the engine of the MGA was a fine performer in its day, it should not be expected to provide the power output or torque of a modern engine. Even so, it should be capable of producing something close to its original specification, though often one of the reasons it doesn't is that things like carburettor spindles are worn, compressions are down because of a combination of worn bores and

Cleaned down, weak metal replaced or reinforced and stripped of all old paint,
the basic body shell is now ready for paint preparation.

piston rings or sloppy valve guides, cylinder head gaskets leak oil (which is one reason why the engine compartment is often in such a sound condition – the oil film coats much of the bodywork and chassis in that area) or the valve seats and heads are so badly burned that the maintenance of compression becomes impossible.

As long as the main structural components of the engine are in sound condition, there's really no reason why the power unit, of whichever type, can't be brought back to its former glory, though it could be at a price if the engine needs a total rebuild. Coming back to the minor solutions though, it's worth checking those carburettor spindles for wear and if they are found to have more than five thousands of an inch play, then you've found one significant cause of power loss. The spindles can be replaced or the carburettor bodies re-bushed without too much trouble, but often this is only part of the problem.

Low oil pressure is often a sign of a worn engine and when so is normally accompanied by high oil consumption, blue exhaust smoke and a generally oily engine compartment. If this is what you face with your newly acquired MGA, then you're in for an engine overhaul. On the other hand, if there's no cold-start rumble from the bottom end of the engine, it's just possible that the low oil

177

pressure might be due to a worn pressure relief valve and compressed valve spring. The pressure valve cap may have wear on the seating face and if it does, replace it. Similarly, if the spring is compressed (measuring less than 3in (75mm) in length), replace it and your oil pressure problems *could* be over. If that proves to be the case, then you might escape with a top-end overhaul to cure the oil consumption problem, focussing attention on the camshaft bearings and valve guides.

The cylinder head of the pushrod engines is a component that merits close inspection, for it is prone to cracks. Oddly enough, even though the engine may well be running quite well, there could be cracks around the valve seats and in the exterior casting between numbers two and three cylinders. While valve seat cracks, if not too deep, can be resolved by the fitment of new valve seats, others may not be too easy to deal with and the only sensible recommendation if the owner is in doubt is to replace the head, as it is possible to buy replacements for the 1500 and both versions of 1600, already fitted with valve guides.

Worn camshaft bearings are a key source of oil pressure loss in the pushrod engine and the obvious cure is to replace them, though if the bearings are worn, the camshafts also warrant close inspection. Replacements can be obtained from leading parts suppliers, such as Moss Europe, and so the problem is not beyond recovery. If oil pressure is restored and blue smoke still comes out of the exhaust, you still have some work to do. If that smoke is there all the time the engine is running, suspect worn valve guides, with oil running down between the valve stem and guide and into the combustion chamber as the inlet valve opens. It's easy enough to replace the valve guides, driving them through to the combustion chamber side of the head, though of course the cylinder head has to be removed to do the job and while you're at it, you'll need to check those valve

seats. It's also sensible to replace the valves and grind those into place after fitting your new valve guides.

If, however, you're faced with sporadic exhaust smoke, showing itself after the engine has been idling and then accelerated, the problem points to piston rings and worn cylinder bores. At this point you can resign yourself to facing a major overhaul, for if the rings are worn on an engine of this age, the chances are the bores are worn, too. If the cylinder bores are at their maximum, you face fitting new cylinder liners and this is the stage at which you decide whether you have the equipment and skills to do it yourself or entrust your engine to a specialist. The latter is usually the wiser course, not least for the preservation of peace of mind and for the fact that somebody else carries the can if something goes wrong.

There is a substantial range of spare parts available for most MGA models, even the Twin-Cam, though this latter model has less major engine parts available than the pushrod versions. You can buy most of the bits you need for the cylinder head; you can buy camshafts, crankshafts, connecting rods, flywheels, cylinder liners, pistons, carburettor bits and in fact just about anything you need for the mechanical rebuild. Clearly, it comes at a price and you have to decide, preferably before you dip your hand in your pocket to buy the car, whether the combined price of purchase and restoration represents value for money to you and whether it would be a more expensive or a less expensive exercise to buy a restored car from a reputable dealer. Of course, if you already own the car, the question is simplified to one of: 'Do I do it myself or give the job to a specialist?'

CHASSIS AND TRANSMISSION

Nine times out of ten, the chassis on an MGA will have something that needs attention. It can range from minor shunt damage to a botched major accident repair. You can even, in the extreme case, be faced with the front end of one chassis mated to the back end of another – that may not be a problem if the 'surgery' has been done skilfully, with substantial tubular reinforcement inside the mated sections and each section carefully cut to provide an accurate set of original dimensions and alignment. Unfortunately, too few chassis are done like that and it does take a high degree of expertise to do such a job properly. So if you suspect your potential purchase is a hybrid, you might be wise to walk away from it, though you may not know it until it's too late.

If you have the chassis stripped and standing on your garage floor, it will be wise, to say the least, to check its alignment and any distortion. A good way of doing this is to set four rigid supports (either axle stands or purpose-made blocks) of as precisely the same height as you can make them, standing about a metre off the floor, upon which you set the chassis frame. Each block or stand should be as near to each corner as you can set it and, presuming your garage floor is flat and your axle stands or pedestals are of the same height all round, you'll soon see whether your chassis has any twist in it. The next thing is to see if it's straight. To check this, simply take two long pieces of string and measure from each front corner of the frame to each opposite rear corner. If the two distances are the same, then your frame is almost certainly OK. But as an added precaution, check the measurements to both the front and rear corners, in the same fashion, from the top corners of the scuttle bridge. If you still have doubts, then consult an expert.

As any car gets older, it is inevitable that the gearbox will whine in the intermediate gears, there may be the odd 'snick' in changing from one low gear to another, giving signs of tired synchromesh (especially on second). MGA rear axles seem to take a remarkable

amount of neglect and abuse and, bearing in mind how few people check the engine oil at proper intervals in cars, it may well be that the gearbox and rear axle oil levels are low, on the 'out-of-sight, out-of-mind' principle. Hub oil seals often need replacing and topping up levels may well highlight this problem, by depositing oil on the brake shoes. If there's already oil on the brake shoes, you'll now know the cause if you didn't before. But whatever you do, be very wary of using oil additives as any form of life-extender, for no additive, whatever claims may be made for it, can actually compensate for badly worn components or seals, however good it might be thought to be. It will be less expensive in the long run to face the overhaul cost for the gearbox, but unless the rear axle has been damaged by extensive driver abuse in its former life, it is likely not to be a major problem.

FINISH AND TRIM

This book is not designed to be a restoration guide. There are plenty of such books on the market now, written by people who have long experience of the MGA and all its foibles. From these you can glean what is correct and original from what is not. And if you want your MGA to become a *concours d'elegance* machine rather than a bit of fun, then you're going to have dig into your pocket for one of those guides. But look through them carefully to ensure that what you want is in there. There is a list of factory colours within these pages, and trim colours, but you should be aware that if a customer turned up at an MG dealership, or at Abingdon, and asked for a particular non-standard colour, the factory would paint the car that non-standard colour, as long as they got paid for it.

You must also recognize that trim parts available today are often slightly different from the originals, because of modified (often

179

MGA COLOUR SCHEMES, COVERING 1500, TWIN-CAM, 1600 MARKS I, II AND DE LUXE

Model	Body Colour	Paint Code	Trim	Piping	Hood/Sidescreens
1500R/TC1R	Black/Red dash	BK1	Red	Red	Black/Ice Blue
1500R/TC1R	Black/Green dash	BK1	Green	Green	Black/Ice Blue
1500C/TC1C	Black	BK1	Red	Red	
1500C/TC1C	Black	BK1	Green	Green	
1600R/2R/TC2R	Black/Beige dash	BK1	Beige	Beige	Grey
1600R/2R/TC2R	Black/Red dash	BK1	Red	Red	Grey
1600C/2C/TC2C	Black	BK1	Beige	Beige	
1600C/2C/TC2C	Black	BK1	Red	Red	
1500R/TC1R	Ash Green	GN2	Grey	Grey	Black/Ice Blue
1500R/TC1R	Ash Green	GN2	Black	Green	Black/Ice Blue
1500C/TC1C	Ash Green	GN2	Grey	Grey	
1500C/TC1C	Ash Green	GN2	Black	Green	
1500R/TC1R	Orient Red	RD3	Red	Red	Black
1500R/1C1R	Orient Red	RD3	Black	Red	Black
1500C/TC1C	Orient Red	RD3	Red	Red	
1500R/1C1C	Orient Red	RD3	Black	Red	
1500R/TC1R	Old English White	WT3	Red	Red	Black
1500R/TC1R	Old English White	WT3	Black	White	Black
1500C/TC1C	Old English White	WT3	Red	Red	
1500C/TC1C	Old English White	WT3	Black	White	
1600R/2R/TC2R	Old English White	WT3	Red	Red	Grey
1600R/2R/TC2R	Old English White	WT3	Black	White	Grey
1600C/2C/TC2C	Old English White	WT3	Red	Red	
1600C/2C/TC2C	Old English White	WT3	Black	White	
1500R/TC1R	Glacier Blue	BU4	Grey	Grey	Black/Ice Blue
1500R/TC1R	Glacier Blue	BU4	Black	Grey	Black/Ice Blue
1500C/TC1C	Island Green	GN6	Grey	Grey	
1500C/TC1C	Island Green	GN6	Black	Green	
1500R/TC1R	Tyrolite Green	GN7	Grey	Grey	Black/Ice Blue
1500R/TC1R	Tyrolite Green	GN7	Black	Green	Black/Ice Blue
1500C/TC1C	Mineral Blue	BU9	Grey	Grey	
1500C/TC1C	Mineral Blue	BU9	Black	Blue	
1600R/2R/TC2R	Alamo Beige	BG9	Red	Red	Red
1600C/2C/TC2C	Alamo Beige	BG9	Red	Red	
1600R/2R/TC2R	Iris Blue	BU12	Black	Lt Blue	Blue
1600C/2C/TC2C	Iris Blue	BU12	Black	Lt Blue	
1600R/2R/TC2R	Chariot Red	RD16	Red	Red	Beige
1600R/2R/TC2R	Chariot Red	RD16	Beige	Beige	Beige
1600R/2R/TC2R	Chariot Red	RD16	Black	Black	Grey
1600C/2C/TC2C	Chariot Red	RD16	Red	Red	
1600C/2C/TC2C	Chariot Red	RD16	Beige	Beige	
1600C/2C/TC2C	Chariot Red	RD16	Black	Red	
1600R/2R/TC2R	Dove Grey	GR26	Red	Red	Grey
1600C/2C/TC2C	Dove Grey	GR26	Red	Red	

KEY:		
	1500R	= 1500 Roadster
	1500C	= 1500 Coupé
	TC1R	= Twin-Cam Roadster with 1500-type body (up to No. 2192)
	TC1C	= Twin-Cam Coupé with 1500-type body (up to No. 2291)
	1600R	= 1600 Mark I Roadster
	1600C	= 1600 Mark I Coupé
	TC2R	= Twin-Cam Roadster with 1600-type body (after No. 2193)
	TC2C	= Twin-Cam Coupé with 1600-type body (after No. 2292)
	2R	= 1600 Mark II Roadster
	2C	= 1600 Mark II Coupé

simplified) manufacturing techniques. In fact, that statement doesn't just apply to trim components, since body panels aren't always made exactly as the originals either. But they are made to fit and will replace the original component without problems. One of the reasons that many of these components don't exactly match the shape is because the tools with which they are made are produced to a price, since the quantities involved don't come anywhere near the manufactured volumes of the original producers – and price is a consideration for the enthusiast.

Paintwork is not generally a process for the amateur, so finishing off your MGA is a process you are well advised to entrust to a specialist. The price of a good paint job is, like mechanical rebuilds, a bit of a lottery. It has often been said that you only get what you pay for and there's a significant amount of truth in that, but it's still possible to be taken for a ride, so you need to use a painter who knows what he's doing; ideally you should seek advice from people who have experience of using good painters whose preparation work is truly capable of protecting your valuable asset for as long as possible. It is prudent, too, to undertake the paint job *before* the interior trim is complete, so that you have trim overlapping paint, not paint overlapping trim.

Interior trim and badges are quite important to the final appearance of a car, so it would be wrong to use cheap substitutes for original items. As an example, it's very easy to be tempted to replace leather with vynide upholstery, but the result would show quite quickly and the car would look less than it should. The durability, the feel and the quality of the original leather trim is undeniable and belongs with the MGA, just as do the correct badges. The only two justifiable reasons for replacing the original chrome trim items with modern reproductions are that they are so damaged as to be unrepairable or that they are missing. Most items can be carefully removed if they are intact in the first place and similarly, most items can be re-plated if they need it. There are quite a lot of sympathetic chrome and nickel platers around today who can work magic with even the smallest items, so don't replace them just because they look a little shabby.

YOUR MGA ON THE ROAD

However much money you've spent on bringing your MGA to the stage where you're about to proudly venture forth on to the highways, it will no doubt represent a substantial investment to you. Having made that investment, you will now want to get the best out of it, whichever variant of MGA it is. One thing that is extremely important in keeping any of these models up to scratch is to follow

181

Looking from rear to front, this is Geoff Barron's bodyshell rust-protected and ready for finish paint.

maintenance routines rigidly. So many classic cars cover low mileages and so are rarely maintained. This is a serious mistake, as it must be remembered that the service intervals for most of these cars were much shorter than the service interval for a modern car. The 10,000-mile service interval was unheard of in the 1950s, in fact many cars needed attention of some kind every 1,000 miles.

A significantly worthwhile investment for your car is an owner's handbook and a workshop manual, because between them, they will give you all the essential information about care and maintenance of your valuable charge. Reprints of both are available, published by Brooklands Books, and they are

exact facsimiles of the originals. From these, you will be able to glean such important data as frequencies of oil changes, routine checks, the dimensions and running clearances essential to the well-being of the mechanical components, tyre pressures (which can vary between different tyre types and even makes) and all the other things that form part of the process of making a car run smoothly.

Because these cars are so much older than the car you drive every day, it is the more important to take notice of what is recommended for their maintenance. Just because oil technology and metallurgy have advanced apace since the 1950s, and your modern car doesn't need servicing as frequently as a

After many long hours of hard work, this is the finished result, a car interior many a manufacturer would be proud to put into a showroom.

consequence of these advances, don't be fooled into thinking that your MGA can be serviced as infrequently, too. As a result of long service intervals, many modern car drivers neglect even the simplest routines which have not been surpassed by technology. These include checking coolant and oil levels at least once a week and tyre pressures once a week. Then, at the risk of seeming repetitious, do follow the service recommendations of the handbooks. Use specialists for anything you can't honestly handle yourself and your car will reward you with years of fun.

Having laboured the maintenance issues, it is fair to say that you can have a huge amount of enjoyment from a well-maintained MGA – and you don't have to nurse it along the road as though it was an invalid. Road tests have proved that the braking ability of the car is well able to handle the performance and if you've followed all the rules in bringing your car back up to scratch, then there's no reason why you can't use that performance capability to the full on modern roads. There's little more depressing than the sight of a fine sports car like an MGA pottering along a Class A road or motorway at about 50mph (80km/h). If you want a sports car because it's a sports car, then drive it like a sports car.

Many people have said that to drive a classic sports car in modern traffic conditions is difficult because of higher average road speeds and better braking performances.

MGA PRODUCTION DATA

Model	Production Period	Number Manufactured (Chassis No.)
MGA 1500	September 1955 to May 1959	10101 to 68,850
MGA Twin-Cam	September 1958 to June 1960	501 to 2611
MGA 1600*	May 1959 to April 1961	6,851 to 100,351
MGA 1600 Mk II	April 1961 to June 1962	100,352 to 109,070

*The MGA De Luxe was built from the remaining Twin-Cam chassis that were left over after Twin-Cam production had ceased. These cars were numbered along with the 1600 and 1600 Mk II chassis numbers, and the actual production numbers of them are generally believed to be 82 '1600' models and 313 '1600 Mk II' models, a total of 395 vehicles.

MGA ENGINE SERIAL NUMBER DATA

To identify MGA engines from their serial numbers, the following table should be used. **Note the early 1500 engines had the serial numbers prefixed by BP.**

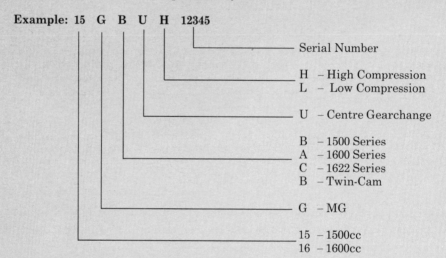

Example: 15 G B U H 12345

- Serial Number
- H – High Compression
- L – Low Compression
- U – Centre Gearchange
- B – 1500 Series
- A – 1600 Series
- C – 1622 Series
- B – Twin-Cam
- G – MG
- 15 – 1500cc
- 16 – 1600cc

CHASSIS NUMBERS

Chassis number for the Twin-Cam are very different to those used on the 1500. Use the following chart to decode your chassis number:

Example: YD1–501 is a RHD Home Market Tourer

YD1	RHD	Home Market Tourer		YM1	RHD	Home Market Coupé
YD2	RHD	Export Market Tourer		YM2	RHD	Export Market Coupé
YD3	LHD	Export Market Tourer		YM3	LHD	Export Market Coupé

There were some other chassis number prefixes, but these were used on CKD exported cars for final assembly overseas. Example YD5–929.

From Moss Europe comes this production data chart, based on original information, and which can help the would-be MGA owner identify his or her new car and locate serial numbers of the major components.

MGA 1500

Chassis numbers for the 1500 are loaded with information about the car. For example HDA 13 10101 tells us that the car is an MGA, two seater, painted in black cellulose for the RHD home market. Use the following chart to decode your chassis number:

Example:

H	D	A	1	3	10101
MGA	2 Seats	Black	RHD Home	Cellulose	Car Number

1st Letter Make H MGA	2nd Letter Model D Tourer M Coupé	3rd Letter Colour A Black D Mineral Blue E Island Green H CKD Finish K Orient Red L Glacier Blue R Old English White T Ash Green U Tyrolite Green	1st Number Market 1 RHD Home 2 RHD Export 3 LHD 4 North America 5 CKD RHD 6 CKD LHD	2nd Number Paint Type 1 Synthetic 2 Synthetic 3 Cellulose 4 Metallic 5 Primed 6 Cellulose Body & Synthetic Wings

MGA 1600, 1600 Mk II

These cars did not provide as much information in their chassis numbers as did the previous models. There are, however, three pieces of information can be extracted from the chassis numbers to identify whether the car is a tourer or coupé, RHD or LHD and finally whether the car is a Mk II.

Example:

G	H	D	L	2	103779
MGA	1600	Coupé	LHD	Mk II	Car Number

1st Letter G MGA	2nd Letter H 1400cc–1900cc	3rd Letter N Tourer D Coupé	4th Letter Blank RHD L LHD	5th Prefix Blank 1600 2 1600 Mk II	6th Number Car Number

The motorway speed limit in Britain today is only 70mph (112km/h). This kind of speed is at the lower end of the optimum performance of the MGA and the non-motorway 60mph (96km/h) is almost uncomfortably low, so there really is no reason why you can't enjoy your MGA in the way it was intended to be enjoyed when it was first built.

The MGA was and is a fine car, well designed, sturdily built and still a good looking machine. Give it the care and attention it deserves and it will reward you with thousands of miles of pleasure at quite modest running costs. There are special insurance schemes available to keep that element of cost down to a realistic minimum: there are specialist parts suppliers and manufacturers to keep it mechanically and bodily fit, and there are specialist workshops who will undertake anything from an oil change to a major restoration. Then there are the clubs – join one and your enjoyment will almost certainly be enhanced.

MGA Clubs

As far as possible, the names and addresses given here are accurate at the time of this book going to press. However, because names and places change frequently, in the event of difficulty, the reader is advised to contact the main club headquarters to verify the name of any local or overseas representative. The MG Car Club publishes, in its magazine *Safety Fast*, a list of over seventy names and addresses for representatives all over the world. That list is too extensive to include here so, with kind permission of the Club, here are the names of the principal overseas regional representatives and centres for the MG Car Club:

GREAT BRITAIN:

The MG Car Club Limited,
Kimber House,
P. O. Box 251,
Abingdon,
Oxfordshire OX14 1PF

The MGA Register,
Geoff Barron,
38 Lily Hill Road,
Bracknell,
Berkshire

The MGA Twin-Cam Register,
Nick Cox,
18 Orchard Drive,
Wooburn Green,
Buckinghamshire HP10 0QN

The MG Owners Club,
Cambridge CB4 1BR

OVERSEAS DIRECTOR OF THE MGCC

Alan Kingwell,
Huntingdon,
19 Olivers Bannery Road,
Winchester,
Hampshire SO22 4JR,
England

EUROPE

John Hale,
Beech Garth,
Parton Road,
Churchdown,
Gloucester GL3 3JH,
England

AUSTRALIA/NEW ZEALAND

Gerald Sweatman,
26 Delves Close,
Ringmere,
Nr Lewes,
East Sussex BN8 5JW,
England

NORTH AND SOUTH AMERICA

Bill & Heather Charlton,
188 Lynwood Drive,
Marley,
Wimborne,
Dorset BH21 1UT,
England

CANADA

MG Car Club of Toronto,
Keith Holdsworth,
P. O. Box 64,
Station R,
Toronto,
Ontario M4C 3Z3,
Canada

North American MGA Register,
Len Bonnay,
528 Alan Avenue,
Welland,
Ontario L3C 2Y9,
Canada
(covering Canada and USA)

UNITED STATES OF AMERICA

MGA Twin-Cam Registry,
Lyle York,
5105 Kingswood Lane,
Anderson,
Indiana 46011,
USA

ASIA

Brian Moyse,
18 Cater Gardens,
Guildford,
Surrey CU2 2BY,
England

AFRICA AND ELSEWHERE

Brian Woodhams,
The Post Office,
19 St Peters Street,
Duxford,
Cambridge CB2 4RP,
England

In addition to those listed above, there are numerous MG clubs throughout the United States. A letter to the MG Car Club at Abingdon will quickly put you in contact with your local organization.

Index